"Barbara and I have great respect for the exemplary life Norman Brinker has led. His life [as depicted in *On the Brink*] has inspired me as it has so many others."

GEORGE BUSH
Forty-first President of the United States

"The life story of Norman Brinker is a must for people of all ages. It is one of how character is built over a lifetime with such cardinal principles as hard work, honesty, integrity and, above all, compassion for and fairness to people. These qualities have made him a beloved leader, and explain why all the challenges that he faced proved so successful."

MAX FISHER

"Leave it to Norman Brinker to add not just a new chapter to a lifetime of leadership achievement, but an entire book of real insight into his winning, 'make-things-happen' style."

ROGER A. ENRICO
CEO, PepsiCo, Inc.

"Norman Brinker is bold enough to live well through the worst adversity that chance can throw at him. This has always amazed his friends and given us heart. It has made his life an ongoing act of kindness."

TOMMY LEE JONES

On the Brink clearly demonstrates why Norman Brinker has been an inspiration to many people over his lifetime."

CHRIS EVERT

"Norman Brinker is the Horatio Alger story incarnate. He once described Chili's as embodying: "Quality, consistency, ambience, and a clear image wrapped in a way that clearly sets you apart from your competition." That is a superb description of Norman Brinker himself. Learning more about him will help all of us to better ourselves."

HERBERT KELLEHER
Chairman of the Board, President and CEO Southwest Airlines

On the Brink provides an insightful perspective on Norman's courage and convictions. He is truly an inspiration to those who have had the good fortune to be associated with him."

RON MCDOUGALL
President and CEO Brinker International

"I've always had a great deal of admiration for Norman Brinker. *On the Brink* is an inspiring journey through a life that exemplifies the essence of American spirit."

RAYMOND FLOYD
Professional golfer

"Norman Brinker is a dreamer and a doer. His inspiring leadership, strength of character and indomitable spirit prove the American dream is alive and well–and living in Texas. I am proud to call Norman a friend."

GEORGE W. BUSH
Governor of Texas

"On the Brink...is an absolutely brilliant personal blueprint for success...[Norman Brinker's] formula of human decency with a strong business acumen and ultimate tenacity makes him a hero and role model for all of us to revere. He did it all for his family, country, community, and church."

RON KIRK
Mayor, Dallas, Texas

"On the Brink lets you live the story of a remarkable man with an incredible legacy–a legacy of individual courage, triumph, integrity, and character. You will be enriched by reading this book."

J.E. OESTERREICHER
Vice Chairman and CEO J.C. Penney Company, Inc.

"The leadership principles contained in *On the Brink* are timeless–they apply to business, athletics, and life in general. Brinker and Phillips have combined to create a compelling story of hope and inspiration. A superb book."

TOM LANDRY
Former head coach, Dallas Cowboys

"Much of Norman Brinker's business success can be attributed to teamwork and caring. *On the Brink* is a must read for all young people who may be searching for the key to a successful life. I heartily recommend it."

TONY DORSETT
NFL Hall of Fame Running Back, Chairman, Touchdown Products

"Norman Brinker has been an inspiration to me and everyone who knows him. *On the Brink* chronicles his remarkable life, which will become a model for everyone who reads it."

MIKE VANCE
Former Dean of Disney University and Chairman of the Creative Thinking Association of America

"If I read [*On the Brink*] and used it as a guide thirty years ago...I could have become really famous."

LARRY HAGMAN

"Norman's uncanny skill of reading the market place, combined with his superior understanding of people sets him apart and above everyone else."

J. MICHAEL JENKINS
President, Vicorp Restaurants, Inc.

"I'm keeping *On the Brink* in my desk drawer to refer to many underlined portions frequently. There's some great wisdom here."

HAROLD SIMMONS
Chairman of the Board, Valhai

"*On the Brink* will keep you forever from the brink. It's a true "life"-saver, a wonderful book."

JOAN VAN ARK
Actress

"*On the Brink* should help even the most conservative individual to become a risk-taker."

STANLEY MARCUS

"I couldn't put it down, it captivated me from the beginning. Norman Brinker is an incredible man who has had a remarkable life. His book is an inspiration."

LYNDA CARTER

"Norm Brinker's life is a great American success story. Determination, energy, intelligence, and never giving in—that's the remarkable character of this remarkable man. He's a true role model for people of all ages, and someone I am proud to count as a friend."

DAN QUAYLE
Former Vice President of the United States

"If you are down and out...knocked off your feet...not sure what hit you...then this book is for you!"

JOHN MACKOVIC
Head Football Coach, University of Texas

"Norman Brinker's leadership principles—including vision, integrity, taking risks, and caring—are timeless. By reading *On the Brink,* you will feel the magic that is the man."

LOU NEEB
Chairman and CEO, Casa Olé Restaurants

"Norman Brinker is an extraordinary human being. His vision, his ability to recruit incredibly talented people, his entrepreneurial instincts and his leadership qualities make him one of the most respected and admired businessmen in America. For those of us who are fortunate enough to know Norman on a personal level, his kindness, warmth, courage and integrity are truly his greatest attributes..."

PHYLLIS GEORGE

"*On the Brink* provides a window into a great leader whom only a few of us have been privileged to know well. The reader will quickly understand how one man can make a difference in the lives of thousands of people."

RICHARD B. BERMAN
President, Berman and Company

"[*On the Brink* depicts] an inspiring life of an inspiring man captured in an inspiring written form."

HERMAN CAIN
Chairman and CEO , Godfather's Pizza, Inc.

"We are thankful that Norman created the opportunities. He encouraged us to innovate, take on responsibilities greater than our experiences and supported us with his incredible resources. Norman is our superhero."

CHRIS SULLIVAN
Chairman and CEO, Outback Steakhouse, Inc.

"If you were to go out and apply Norman's leadership principles to a business, there are no limits to what you can accomplish."

BOB BASHAM
Co-founder, Outback Steakhouse, Inc.

"Reading this book is almost as powerful as being with Norman Brinker. It is the remarkable story of the most remarkable recovery of the most remarkable man I have ever known. You'll be inspired—and likely changed."

TRAMMELL CROW
Founder, Trammell Crow Company

"*On the Brink* is a tremendous story that illustrates great accomplishments. Norman Brinker is an incredible inspiration for all on what we can do and accomplish if we just stay the course."

J. IRA HARRIS
Senior Managing Director Lazard Freres & Co., LLC

"If you seek success in business and life—read this book. Norman's leadership has transformed the food service industry, just as it has the lives of us fortunate enough to have worked with him."

DICK RIVERA
President, Longhorn Steaks, Inc.

"Norm Brinker is a winner, and he can teach you how to be one, too. The life skills you will learn from him can increase your success and also give you the internal strength to rise up from an unexpected event that knocks you on your ear. You'll learn why leadership starts on the inside."

KEN BLANCHARD
Co-author, The One-Minute Manager

"Norman Brinker is one of my heroes. He is a man of integrity. he is honest, and he does know his potatoes from his carrots when it comes to putting together a right-good eatery. He is also tougher than the back wall of a shooting gallery. Nothing can keep him down for long. He is a winner."

LARRY GATLIN
Singer/Songwriter and former Steak & Ale waiter

"Time and time again, Norman Brinker's leadership principles have demonstrated proven results in the world of athletics—where a team must be inspired to work both together and perform individually. Brinker and Phillips provide us with some great leadership lessons. Every young person should read *On the Brink.*"

JOE PATERNO
Head Football Coach, Penn State University

"Norman Brinker is pure inspiration. he shows humanity, the ways to achieve the respect and integrity [that help] elevate all involved. I loved the read, and now I want to run out and practice what Norman has shared."

LINDA GRAY
President, Linda Gray Productions

On the Brink

On the Brink

The Life and Leadership of Norman Brinker

by
Norman Brinker
and
Donald T. Phillips

THE SUMMIT PUBLISHING GROUP • ARLINGTON, TEXAS

THE SUMMIT PUBLISHING GROUP
One Arlington Centre, 1112 East Copeland Road, Fifth Floor
Arlington, Texas 76011

Copyright © 1996 by Norman Brinker and Donald T. Phillips

Printed in the United States of America.
95 96 97 98 99   010   5 4 3 2 1

Library of Congress Cataloging-in-Publication Data

Brinker, Norman, 1931-
    On the brink : the life and leadership of Norman Brinker/ by Norman Brinker and Donald T. Phillips.
        p. cm.
    Includes index.
    ISBN 1-56530-212-5
    1. Brinker, Norman, 1931-   . 2. Restaurateurs–United States–Biography.   I.
Phillips, Donald T. (Donald Thomas), 1952-   . II. Title.
TX910.5.B69A3   1996
647.95'092–dc20
    [B]   96-13412
                                                                         CIP

Cover and book design by David Sims

For Kathryn and Gene,
my mother and father;

For Cindy, Brenda, and Eric,
my children; and

Especially for Nancy,
my wife, my love.

NORMAN BRINKER

~

This one's for Norman.

DON PHILLIPS

CONTENTS

....

This book is about determination, perseverance, and putting into practice key leadership principles that have proved over and over again to work both in business and in personal life. It is also a book about recovery, inspiration, and hope.

In January 1993, I was involved in a polo accident from which I very nearly died. It was, of course, one of the most traumatic events of my life. The majority of doctors who attended me believed I would not live, much less make a full and complete recovery. Likewise, many people doubted I would succeed in business as I have, given my modest beginnings. But hard work and determination, combined with motivation, can and do make a difference.

From a lifetime of experiences, I've concluded that motivation absolutely comes from within—and that leadership can, in fact, be learned if one possesses a certain set of innate traits. The accident really brought this into focus for me because, throughout my recovery process, I used the same principles that I had employed to achieve success in business at Jack-In-The-Box, Steak & Ale, Burger King, Pillsbury, Chili's, and Brinker International. The result has been twenty-eight consecutive years of bottom-line improvement.

Over the years, I've given innumerable presentations on leadership and motivation—and have been frequently asked to write a book about both my leadership philosophy and the details of my accident and subsequent return. This is that book. Now is the right time for it since I've recovered from my injuries and turned over the position of chief executive officer of Brinker International to Ron McDougall, a twenty-three-year associate. I now serve as chairman of the board.

I believe the basic principles we've outlined herein can be very helpful to individuals on a broad basis. People don't have to be powerful figures or possess magic to accomplish a great deal in their lives. But it is important that they have basic integrity, energy, enthusiasm, determination, and perseverance.

My parents, Kathryn and Gene Brinker, taught me that when you possess something that can be of help to others, you should share it. That's why I wrote this book. Hopefully it will be meaningful to many people—both personally and professionally.

My life is an example of how attracting talented, vibrant associates and leaders makes the difference between success and failure. I cannot adequately express my appreciation for the teamwork, energy, and initiative my associates have displayed over the years. It has been ongoing and truly outstanding.

A number of individuals have helped and influenced me during my business career. I would particularly like to acknowledge Stephen Covey for the tremendous impact he had over the decade in which he spent so many hours with me and my team, talking about basic principles of life and leadership. I cannot thank him enough for the significant influence he's had on my thinking.

I'd also like to acknowledge John Beatrice, Morton Feinberg, Mike Vance, and Bob Peterson (my mentor for six years and my first employer)—all of whom have had a major influence on my business success.

Also, a special heartfelt thanks to:

All my friends who were there for me after my accident and during recovery, especially: Steve Bottum, Marjorie and Max Fisher, Isabell and Joe Haggar, Nicki and Ira Harris, Bob Mosbacher, Nancy and Vince Paul, Margot and Ross Perot, and Pat and Pete Schenkel;

The doctors who attended me at a critical time, particularly my good friends Phil Williams and Sandy Carden;

All the therapists who helped me on the road to recovery, especially Erin Fay Azzato, Robyn Stephens Budine, and Shani Unterhalter Romick;

All the employees of Brinker International for their encouragement and support.

Maureen Connolly Brinker, my first wife, was always 100 percent supportive. She is also a part of this story, and I wish, in part, to dedicate this book to Maureen's memory.

I'd like to thank my assistant, Margaret Valentine, who has been with me for many years. Her patience, vitality, and sense of direction are remarkable.

Ellie and Marvin Goodman are the best, most support- ive in-laws one could possibly have. I wouldn't be here today without them.

All my love and gratitude to my two daughters, Cindy and Brenda, whom I used to take in car seats visiting restau- rants, and who have always been there for me; and to my son, Eric, who was supportive every step of the way during the accident and recovery.

And finally, all my love to Nancy, who has been a tremendous supporter in all ways; and who deserves special thanks for bringing me back from the brink of death to the joy of life with her by my side.

NORMAN BRINKER
April, 1996

～

I first met Norman Brinker in mid-April of 1995. He was looking for some advice on speech writing when a mutual friend recommended we get together. During that initial one-hour meeting, Norman expressed an inter- est in my first book, *Lincoln on Leadership*. He listened intently as I explained my views of leadership and the details of how Abraham Lincoln had led the United States during the Civil War.

For some reason, Norman took a real interest in me, and began talking about a book he and I might write together. I immediately liked him, as well, but was a bit reserved about entering into a massive project on the spur of the moment with someone I really didn't know. We ended the meeting with an agreement to get to know each other a little better.

A few days later, Norman called me and said: "Hi, Don. I'm really anxious to get started on our book." It was obvious that he had already decided it was a done deal–and I just couldn't turn him down, because he was so darned sincere about it. So, over the next several weeks, I did some research and spent a considerable amount of time with him. And to make a long story short, I came to the conclusion that his was a story that needed to be told and told well. But it took me six weeks to decide what Norman had decided within forty-five minutes of our first meeting–that we were going to write a book together. When I told Norman of my decision, he just smiled.

In the 1980s and 1990s, a great deal was written about economies of scale, leveraged buyouts, and taking pieces of a company and selling them off. Everything was viewed from a financial point of view. But caught in each of those financial transactions were people–people who made those companies successful, who made them great.

In researching Norman's story, I found that caring about people was a major part of his leadership philosophy. I also noticed that he possessed two personal attributes clearly defined in nearly all great leaders, past and present: a dynamic *sense of achievement* combined with an overwhelming feeling of *compassion* for others. As a result, when Norman built his companies, he always thought first of the people with whom he worked.

Many business people read my earlier book and told me that Abraham Lincoln's leadership style would not work in today's business world. However, Norman Brinker read my book and told me that not only did Lincoln's philosophy work, it also was the same style he had employed in creating his successful businesses–with some extraordinarily strong financial results. In my opinion, he is a living example that managers can be nice to people and still succeed.

By the way, it's worth noting that Norman Brinker is one of the most successful and beloved leaders in business today. Employees at Brinker International do not merely like him—they love him. He often receives sustained standing ovations whenever he speaks to others about his life story. And many people are not content only to shake his hand—they often hug him.

From the structure of this book, one might get the impression that Norman and I worked separately on alternating chapters, which was not the case. We worked together on the entire manuscript in a collaborative effort. Ours was a true partnership—and I'm grateful to Norman for asking me to work with him on this project.

The reader will also quickly notice that Norman Brinker constantly took risks that threatened both his physical and financial well-being. Anyone who takes risks is bound to get hurt eventually, and that certainly happened to Norman a time or two. But the remarkable thing about him is that, whether he was recovering from a horse-riding accident or struggling in business, he just kept coming back, never giving up, never giving in.

After my wife, Susan, read a first draft of one of the early chapters, she turned to me and remarked: "He certainly lived life on the brink, didn't he."

My immediate response was: "What do you mean '*did*'? He still does!"

That's how the title, *On the Brink,* was born.

I'd like to thank Susan, not only for her insight, but also for her love and support throughout the entire process. And thanks to our children, Steve, Dave, and Kate, who made do without Dad on weekends and nights for many months.

Norman and I would also like to thank the following people for their contributions, whether it was through personal interviews, reviews of the manuscript, and/or suggestions for improvement: Stewart Armstrong, John Batrus,

Rick Berman, Marvin Braddock, Brenda Brinker Bottum, Eric Brinker, Nancy Brinker, Dr. Sandy Carden, Harold Deem, Charles Dowaliby, Creed Ford, Ellie and Marvin Goodman, Karen Harrington, Carl Hays, Larry Lavine, Ray Martinez, Ron McDougall, Lou Neeb, George Olivas, Ross Perot, Don Phillips Sr., Susan Phillips, Shani Unterhalter Romick, Cindy Brinker Simmons, CeCe Smith, John Titus, Margaret Valentine, Dr. Phil Williams, Jeff Zucker, and all the people at Summit.

Norman's mother, Kathryn Brinker, kept a daily diary for more than fifty years—spanning the Great Depression and World War II. I had the honor and privilege of reading those diaries. They not only provided invaluable insight into Norman's formative years, they proved to be a compelling legacy from a remarkable and wonderful woman. Kathryn died fifteen years before I was introduced to her son, and, although I never knew her, I will never forget her.

And, finally, I'd like to acknowledge the support and kindness of Nancy Brinker in making this book a reality. I will never forget the tears that came to her eyes in recounting the detailed story of Norman's accident—tears she did not have time to shed while those events were unfolding. I'm convinced she saved Norman's life and, more than any other person, helped bring him back to all of us. She's a remarkable human being; everybody's friend. Thanks, Nancy.

DONALD T. PHILLIPS
April, 1996

CHAPTER

1

.

> *"People often tell me that polo is dangerous. But if they took away the danger, I think I'd just as soon go do something else."*
>
> **NORMAN BRINKER,**
> *1981*

> *"My God, he's not breathing! Get him some oxygen, quick!"*
>
> **NANCY BRINKER,**
> *January 21, 1993*

The Accident

....

Polo had it all for Norman Brinker. All of his natural inclinations and passions came together on twelve acres of land with eight players and eight horses. There was competition, athletics, intellectual activity, anticipation, speed, and always, always going for the goal–striving to achieve, attempting to score.

And there was the risk associated with the game; the very real danger that makes polo one of the few sports that necessitates worrying about getting seriously injured. But it is the poloist's own intelligence and athletic skill that help him negotiate and control the risks involved: Riding at full speed, stopping on a dime and immediately galloping off in another direction; the fast changes and reactions; the split-second timing; hitting a little white ball forward, backward, sideways; or carrying it on a small mallet attached to a thin bamboo shaft–all the while sitting five feet above the ground on a one-thousand-pound horse moving at speeds up to thirty miles an hour. To a very large degree, the poloist is in control of his own destiny. And Norman liked that.

He also loved the art associated with pure horsemanship when steed and rider become one–mystically bonded with grace and beauty, gliding together on the wind. He had always been attracted to horses; almost mesmerized by them, in fact. It was something about the motion, the sound, the feeling of strength. And one thing is certain: Ever since he was five years old, Norman Brinker just wanted to ride—like some people want to fly.

It has been said of polo that, similar to flying, the sport comprises "hours of pure boredom punctuated by moments of sheer terror." This inherent danger has always been one of the central attractions to those who have played the game. General George S. Patton, an avid poloist, once wrote of the sport that: "The element of personal risk is not a drawback but a decided advantage." Activist President Theodore Roosevelt frequently played the game—as did Lord Louis Mountbatten and Winston Churchill.

Polo not only kept Norman Brinker in top physical condition, it also proved to be a needed athletic outlet for releasing all the energy he had inside. Moreover, Norman seemed to be happy on the polo field whether his team won or lost. But while he loved the competition, he would stand on the sidelines whenever an argument or fight occurred—declining to yell at a player or an official.

Those who played with him often commented that Norman was a very enthusiastic, team-oriented player. He was known for his fairness, his consistency, and his excellent horsemanship. Of course, the people who knew him best realized that his skill and his love for horses had won him a berth on the 1952 U.S. Olympic Equestrian Team and in the 1954 Modern Pentathlon World Championships in Budapest, Hungary.

All-in-all, Norm Brinker could hold up his end of the polo field. And like the best athletes of every sport, in a modern polo match he was always around the ball, passing it up the field, slapping it to his teammates, scoring.

The rules of polo are strictly enforced so as to minimize accidents. None more so than the right-of-way rule, which states that a player's direct line to a ball he has just hit may not be crossed. The most serious accidents in polo occur when two half-ton horses collide with each other at a full thirty-mile-an-hour gallop. Only on a horse, the rider has no seat belts or air bags–just a small helmet. The most tragic kind of fall occurs when a horse goes down sideways, and the rider cannot be catapulted out of the saddle. In this worst-case scenario, the horse usually falls on the rider.

The fact is that injuries are part of the sport. Nearly all experienced polo players have been hurt at one time or another. They break arms and legs, crack collarbones, and shatter pelvises. Serious head injuries occur only occasionally. Concussions are more common.

∽

THERE SEEMED TO BE no more risk than usual on Thursday, January 21, 1993, as Chili's began play against Cadillac in the Challenge Cup tournament at the Palm Beach Polo and Country Club in Florida. The game had been postponed more than a week by continuous rains that saturated the area commonly referred to as the "Mecca of United States Polo." And the Brinkers' planned return to Dallas was delayed accordingly, because Norman wasn't about to miss the match.

At last the rains let up, and the clouds blew away to create a beautiful sunny day. It was a fine afternoon for polo. Norman and his teammates, Stewart Armstrong, Fortunato Gomez, and George Olivas, took to the field with their typical enthusiasm–although Norman seemed slightly distracted and a bit weary from all the waiting.

The match began very competitively, but it was somewhat sluggish because the field was still wet. At the conclusion of the second chukker, Chili's led Cadillac by a single goal (3-2) in a low-scoring contest–and many of the horses were tiring noticeably from the heavy field conditions.

Stewart Armstrong changed his mount during the break–and Norman switched to a small but quick horse named Kachobie.

Nancy Brinker arrived minutes before the third chukker began. She parked her four-wheel-drive Land Cruiser at midfield and climbed up on the roof for a good view. After surveying the crowd for a few moments, she spotted her husband just as the whistle blew and play stopped when a horse kicked up a dirt clod that lodged squarely in Norman's left eye. After dismounting and grabbing a towel to wipe away the mud, he got back on his horse and glanced briefly in her direction. Nancy waved to catch his attention as he trotted out to resume play, but he didn't see her.

When the game picked up, the Cadillac team, led by Joe Henderson, began to take control of the ball and drive it toward Chili's goal. Henderson was ranked an eight, and, at six-feet, three-inches tall and two-hundred pounds, he was also one of the largest and strongest men playing modern polo. He rode a huge horse that stood sixteen hands high.

Riding to the left side of the field as he approached the goal, Henderson attempted to hit a cut shot to the right at a forty-five-degree angle to the ball. Norman was riding around from his defensive position, trying to anticipate the shot when Henderson slightly mishit the ball, propelling it right underneath Kachobie. Instinctively, Norm tried to turn his mount back toward his own goal in an attempt to hit a nearside back-shot and drive the ball up the field. Because the ball was slightly mishit, Norman instantly found himself between Henderson and the ball–technically a foul.

Henderson and Norman were both galloping at high speed. Kachobie did not turn to the right as quickly as he should have–and before Henderson knew it, he was right on top of Norman. In that brief moment, Norman got "T-boned" (a common polo term for a broadside impact) from the left side as he was leaning over trying to strike at the ball on his right side. He never saw what hit him.

Eyewitnesses to the accident said that the impact was powerful and frightening. And most agreed that it was one of those plays that happened so fast it was almost impossible to avoid. They cited a series of unusual circumstances: the mishit shot by Henderson; the heavy field conditions; Kachobie's slow reaction time; Norman's vision perhaps slightly impaired on his left side; and the instinct of two highly competitive and aggressive riders striving to reach the ball.

The larger size and weight of Henderson's horse knocked Norman and his horse down sideways—the worst possible collision. There was nowhere to escape. Norman was driven into the ground with the full force of the initial high-speed collision and the additional weight of his own mount. The right side of his head smashed into the ground and he was knocked out instantly. Kachobie fell on him and was momentarily stunned. When the horse recovered and tried to get up, she again rolled over on Norman, crushing some ribs in the process.

Officials immediately blew the whistle and signaled a severe accident. Play was stopped, never to be resumed. Henderson, Armstrong, and Gomez quickly jumped off their horses and rolled Kachobie over on her back so as not to strike Norman again. Friends, players, staff at the polo club, and bystanders all rushed to the scene. Some well-intentioned individual rolled Norman over and took off his helmet.

Norman was lying on his back, eyes rolling around in his head, with a pale gray color in his face. Armstrong reached down to take Norman's pulse, but was so shaken up he couldn't stop his hand from trembling. Ed Bernard, a spectator and longtime Brinker friend, helped take the pulse. It was a strong seventy-eight—excellent considering the trauma involved.

Big Joe Henderson, whose quick reaction helped prevent further injury to Norman, stood quietly to the side holding Kachobie—worried, nervous, feeling awful about the accident.

At center field, about a hundred yards away, Nancy Brinker sat stunned for a few seconds. Usually when Norman fell, he would let her know he was okay by waving an arm or jumping right up—even if he had a broken bone. This time she saw no movement whatsoever—and it frightened her.

She jumped off the roof of the car and started running across the field to the accident—wishing later that she had driven the car. Both Nancy and a small medical vehicle with two attendants got to Norman at the same time—which was about a minute after the fall. At that point, he was having some seizures and turning blue. Nancy, no stranger to medical emergencies, knew that the first three minutes after a traumatic accident could well make the difference between life and death.

"My God," she screamed, "he's not breathing. Get him some oxygen, quick! And bring me the board. We've got to immobilize him fast." The medics responded that the door on their van was locked, and they didn't know where the oxygen was.

"Please hurry," pleaded Nancy.

Finally they found the small oxygen bags and brought them out. "We don't know how to activate these things," said one medic. Nancy activated the oxygen while the medic cleared Norman's mouth. Once they strapped on the oxygen, the seizures stopped, and he began to breathe normally.

Someone mentioned they had called for an ambulance, but Nancy said that wouldn't do. It would take at least thirty minutes for one to arrive on the scene. She immediately determined to get Norman to the nearest emergency room, which was about fifteen minutes away.

"Load him in the van," she told the medic, "we're taking him over to the local hospital."

"I can't transport a patient," he responded. "It's against the state law."

At that point, Nancy felt a surge of adrenaline and assumed a boxer's position with fists raised. "Screw the state law," she screamed. "Just get him in there, and I'll assume the responsibility and take the consequences."

The medics put Norman in their vehicle.

Only four to six minutes passed from the moment of the collision to the time he was on his way to Wellington Regional Hospital. Nancy followed behind in her Land Cruiser—all the while honking the horn in an attempt to alert traffic. With a mobile phone, Nancy called Dr. Sandy Carden, a family friend at St. Mary's Medical Center in Palm Beach. Luckily, he was in his office when she called.

"Sandy," she cried. "Norman's been hurt. He's unconscious. I'm terrified. We're taking him over to the emergency room at the local hospital. I'll get him to St. Mary's as soon as possible. Can you get a neurosurgeon to meet me there when we arrive? Please help us."

After she hung up the phone, Nancy felt that Wellington Regional might not respond to Norman's immediate needs quickly and efficiently because of its size. That was a chance she felt she just couldn't take. While she was not a doctor, Nancy knew enough medical lingo to get by. So she decided to fib.

When they arrived, she sprinted in front of her husband's gurney. A male nurse opened the doors, and Nancy's authoritative voice rang out: "I'm Dr. Brinker," she stated. "This is my patient. Code Blue! This is a Code Blue! He's in extreme distress. Take him to the ICU. Get him intubated. Staff! Let's move!"

"Yes, Doctor," was the immediate response.

Nancy followed Norman into the Intensive Care Unit to make sure he was receiving the best treatment possible. He was. And Nancy was comforted. The hospital staff quickly put him on a respirator. Although he was still unconscious, his color came back, and his condition stabilized.

After rapidly filling out some paperwork, "Dr. Brinker" ordered X rays to find out definitively what they were dealing with. She knew, for instance, that if Norman had a spinal cord injury, he would need a steroid injection right away to minimize damage. When the tests revealed nothing was broken along the spinal cord, a trauma hawk helicopter was summoned for emergency transport to St. Mary's Catholic Hospital in Palm Beach.

Upon arrival at St. Mary's, Dr. Carden was waiting with several specialists, and Norman was immediately taken to the ICU located on the ground floor near the emergency room. The sister in charge came down to meet Nancy and assured her that "Mr. Brinker will get the best treatment possible."

After filling out the necessary paperwork, Nancy was taken in to see Norman. But she was totally unprepared for what she saw.

He was lying flat on his back with legs separated and arms extended. Only a light sheet covered him. There were all kinds of tubes hooked up to his body—a respirator in his mouth, a tube in his left arm, another in his chest, and the usual catheters. And the doctors had drilled a hole in the center of Norman's forehead to hook up an Intracranial Pressure (ICP) monitor to make certain they knew if and when swelling began to occur.

That tube, rising several inches out of his forehead, disturbed Nancy the most. "My God," she wondered. "Is he going to die?"

～

AS THE SITUATION BEGAN to settle down in Norman's hospital room, a harsh reality set in. There didn't seem to be much that anyone could do. And as Nancy sat by the bed holding her husband's hand, a curious routine developed during which there were many hours of pure boredom punctuated by moments of incessant activity. At times, alarms would go off, and hospital attendants would rush in, check him out, and then reset the machines. But most of the time, all that could be heard was the rhythmic "beep, beep, beep" of his heartbeat on the cardiac monitor–and the sound of the respirator as it breathed for him.

For the first time in his life, thought Nancy, Norman Brinker was not in control of his own destiny. He had no say in what was happening to him. This man–who was always so healthy, so robust, a former world-class athlete–was now in a totally helpless position.

Norman did not move at all. He was in a deep coma. And one could only imagine what, if anything, he might have been dreaming about.

2

.

> *"My mother needs the sack."*
>
> **NORMAN BRINKER,**
> *age five*

> *"Little Boy, you have to learn to take care of yourself. You got into it, you get out of it."*
>
> **GENE BRINKER,**
> *to son Norman, age eleven*

> *"Who the hell is Injun Joe?"*
>
> **NORMAN BRINKER,**
> *age seventeen*

The Early Years

There he was—a five-year-old boy with a crew cut and a winsome smile—in an old canvas knapsack up to his armpits. One end of a rope, which held the sack in place, was tied securely around his chest. The other end was tied to a low-hanging tree limb. He was hoisted high enough so that his toes inside the sack were barely touching the ground.

Young Norman Brinker was unable to move—to go where he wanted to go. He felt helpless and frustrated. Yet there was a determined look on his face as he struggled to get free. He bounced around from one point to the other—back and forth, back and forth—as the limb bent under his weight. But the tree was too strong to break, and his hands too weak to untie the rope.

"It was only fifteen minutes, but it felt like forever," he remembered. Finally his mother came up to him. "Well, Norman," said Kathryn Brinker. "Have you learned your lesson?"

"Yes, Mother," came the earnest reply.

"Norman, I had to borrow that sack to teach you that you just can't keep running off. I don't know what else to do with you. You disappear for two or three hours at a time. I don't know where you get to. You could get hurt or God knows what. Now, you are not allowed to run off anymore. Do you understand that, young man?"

"Yes, Mother," he said again.

Norman stayed close to the house for the next few weeks. But one afternoon, Kathryn, with a wary eye, sent him outside to play. And, ever mindful of the punishment should he run off again, the five-year-old just hung around…

…until he saw the horse.

It was tied to a stake, grazing in the field next to their home. Norman just stared and stared at it, as if spellbound.

"I had never taken a ride on a horse before, although it was something I'd been determined to do," recalled Norman. "I knew our next-door neighbors, the Wilsons, owned it—because it was in their field. They were nice people, I thought. They probably wouldn't mind."

Without a second thought, the little boy went out into the field, untied the horse, and led him over to the wooden fence he had just crawled through. He climbed up on the rails and set himself squarely on the horse's back. Then he rode out the open gate and down the dirt road away from his house. As Norman began to get the hang of it, he experienced a sensation he would remember for the rest of his life—riding bareback, the wind in his face, the sound, the motion, the feeling of power.

After a couple of miles, the five-year-old got a little tired. He slid himself down but fell when his feet hit the ground. As he did so, Norman accidentally let go of the halter and watched in horror as the horse ran off.

While he walked back home, reality set in. Because he knew he would be punished, he stopped in at his neighbor's house and knocked on the door. "Why, hello, Norman," said Mrs. McKaughan, the friendly lady who answered. "What can I do for you?"

"My mother needs the sack," he said firmly.

So Mrs. McKaughan went out to the barn, picked up the same knapsack the little boy's mother had returned only a few weeks ago, and gave it to Norman—who began to walk the final half mile or so back home. In a few minutes, he spotted his parents approaching–and could see that his mother, in particular, was unusually angry.

"Norman Brinker," said Kathryn, shaking her finger at him as she approached, "I put you in a bag and tied you to a tree–and you still keep running off. What am I going to do with you?"

"I'm sorry, Mother, I couldn't help myself," he said. "I know you're going to put me in the sack. So, here, I brought it for you. I guess it hasn't cured me yet!"

As little Norman stretched out his arms and held up the canvas knapsack for her, Kathryn melted. She couldn't bear to do it again. And she also realized it was useless to even try. There was something about this youngster that kept him moving. He was a constant whirlwind of activity–curious to the core. She knew now that she would just have to learn to live with it.

"After that," said Norman, "Mother started me on an allowance of seven cents a week–'a penny a day' if I behaved myself. And every few weeks, she would pay fifty cents an hour to let me ride a horse at the nearby riding academy."

Norman, as an unusually active child, would easily get bored. Often he would act impulsively on whatever interested him at the moment. One day in 1936, for instance, his mother recorded in her diary that when she called him for dinner, he replied that he'd be right there. "The next thing I knew," she wrote, "Norman and his little buddy, David, had gone fishing!"

"I remember Mother" said Norm in later years, "sometimes standing on the back porch calling my name. 'NORMAN! NORMAN! Come home this instant,' she'd yell at the top of her lungs."

Through most of his childhood, Norman Brinker also had discipline problems in school–frequently getting into fights and other mischief. While he received A's and B's in most subjects, he consistently got C's and D's in deportment. Norman admitted years later that he had a terrible temper during most of his childhood. "If I saw a guy who was taking advantage of somebody else, I got involved, and it usually resulted in a fight," he explained. "I'd just feel something surge in me that said, 'I've got to take care of that.'"

An example he cited was a kids' baseball game in which one of the bigger boys was running around the bases shoving and pushing the players in the field. "He was strong and mean; he'd push people down—and I didn't like that. So, I went up to him and said: 'That just won't do, fella. No more of that, or we're in trouble.' Naturally, a wrestling match resulted."

"That's the way it usually happened," he continued. "Then, to top it all off, I'd get in trouble with the teacher." One day, the precocious seven-year-old came home from school and proudly reported: "Good news, Mother, I only got talked to three times today. Everybody was really happy. Me, too."

But Kathryn Brinker was well-suited to handle her dynamic little boy. That's because Norman's mom was a bit of a windstorm herself. She was a schoolteacher, a secretary for the local Methodist church, a writer of poems and short stories that received more publisher rejections than acceptances—and she kept a daily diary for more than fifty years. Norman's mother believed, and instilled in her only son, that it was never acceptable just to be doing things only for yourself. She began her 1941 diary by writing this brief poem:

> *'Tis not what we get*
> *But what we give*
> *That measures the worth*
> *Of the life we live.*

She viewed her challenge as one of channeling Norman's energy in the proper direction. Kathryn exposed her curious young son to just about everything. She would, for instance, make him listen to classical music and Milton Cross's opera on the radio every Saturday. "You've got to listen to this because you've got to be rounded," she'd tell Norman. "You must learn to appreciate good music–like Chopin, Mozart, and Handel." Kathryn would also take him to movies, plays, and recitals. And they would play board games and read a variety of books together.

Norman's mother believed in her son completely. She was his strongest and earliest source of encouragement and support. And even though Kathryn was without material luxuries, many of the neighborhood children remembered her as "the nearest thing to a saint" they had ever seen. "She may be poor," neighbor Evelyn Dowaliby once said of Kathryn Brinker, "but there's royalty in that woman."

Norman's father, Eugene Brinker, did not have a college education. Early in life, he worked as a rancher and a cowboy. Later he was employed by the Colorado Highway Department in Denver. It was then, at the age of fifty, that he met and married twenty-eight-year-old Kathryn Payne. A few years after that, in 1931, Norman was born. In the late 1930s, Gene moved his family to Roswell, New Mexico, where he had purchased a ten-acre farm. At that point, he made his living by raising and fattening cattle, and by taking odd jobs as a ranch hand. The family also raised some crops, mainly cotton and alfalfa.

Eugene Brinker was a gentle man–easygoing, people-smart, down-to-earth, likable. In addition to possessing a bit more life experience than most younger fathers, he was uncommonly principle-centered. And, while Kathryn exposed her son to varied cultural activities, Gene made it a point to teach Norman independence and self-reliance. He was also very encouraging.

"Whenever I went up to him and asked if I could try something new," remembered Norman, "Dad would say, 'Why not? Go ahead and do it if you think you can.' Then he'd add: 'But, Little Boy, if you say you are going to do something, you do it. Never take a shortcut and never, ever tell anything but the truth.'"

With an unusual term of affection, Gene Brinker always called his son "Little Boy." In some small way, it may have served to encourage his son's independent nature. But one thing is abundantly clear: Norman's father imbued in him a set of principles that demanded personal responsibility. And his father practiced what he preached.

Norman, for example, never forgot the time he was out working in the alfalfa field when his father came up to him shaking a check. "See this! See this!" said Gene. "This is from the government—for something I should do. It's a subsidy check. They sent me money to pay for my putting concrete under a pump. But that was my responsibility, not theirs."

And, with that, Norman's father ripped the check into pieces. "That's the kind of thing that this government is doing," said Gene Brinker. "Some time in your lifetime, our government will guarantee that they'll take care of you for life. You won't be responsible for yourself. And you know what? You and your children will pay for it."

"The tearing-up of that check made a lasting impression on me," said Norman. "It was worth thirteen dollars—quite a sum of money in the mid-nineteen forties for a poor family who lived day-to-day. My father taught me three very valuable lessons: One, you are only self-limiting. Two, you are self-responsible. And three, if you make a commitment, you must follow through."

Clearly, Norman's parents were very supportive of their only child. They gave him a lot of latitude to attempt anything he wanted to do. He was raised in an environment where people did not snipe at each other; where his parents frequently talked to him about ethics and values; where material things were not thrown at him because there were none to throw. As a result, Norman grew up without emotional or self-esteem problems. He was raised with a deeply instilled set of values, a strict code of ethics—and the encouragement to pursue his dreams. As his mother often said: "Give a lot and demand a lot of yourself. It will all come back with interest."

~

NOT SURPRISINGLY, Norman's first dream was to own a horse. In the first grade, while many of his classmates wanted bicycles, he was pestering Gene and Kathryn for "just one little horse." But because they couldn't afford it, young Norman would run out behind the barn and cry when his friends rode by on their horses. At the same time, he did not want them to know how badly he felt.

"That's when being poor first began to bother me," remembered Norm. "And the feeling intensified when I played with my buddies Teddy and Barry Klingsmith. We all loved to go down and swim in the stream out behind my house. Frequently, Mrs. Klingsmith would drive down to get her boys to go to their country club for activities. Sometimes, they'd invite me, but most of the time they wouldn't. It was during those times that I resolved to one day have enough money to belong to a country club myself—so I would never again be left behind."

Some people didn't mind being poor—but, by the age of nine, Norman Brinker definitely did not like it. What's more, he took concrete action to make money—with the specific goal of owning a horse.

He began by doing odd jobs around the farming community for a few cents here and there. As he saved up his pennies, he would periodically take his piggy bank down the road a few miles to the riding academy. Norman knew that the owner was a horse trader and that there were usually lots of horses around. He'd knock on the door and be ushered into the owner's office. The kindly old gentleman always received him warmly. "Why hello, Norman. How are you today?" he'd ask.

"How much more money do I need for a horse?" inquired the boy as he poured out all his pennies, nickels, and dimes on the desk. "Here's all the money I have," he said. The owner would then smile and gently tell Norman that he didn't have enough yet–but that he could work around the academy to earn some extra money, which he gladly did.

Norman then took several short-time jobs, including picking cotton for a few cents a day. After he had saved up fifteen dollars, he set his sights on a dappled gray gelding named Silver. Norman went to see the horse's owner, who was asking fifty dollars. But the boy's sincerity and his infectious smile enticed Mr. James Dowaliby to agree to let Silver go for thirty dollars–still twice as much as Norman had saved up.

"At this point," said Norman, "my strategy was to persuade my grandmother to lend me the fifteen dollars I needed to buy the horse. She lived in Bloomington, Illinois, and I'd call her every month or so to talk about my desire to own a horse. As phone calls were expensive, I would rehearse what I had to say, and my mother would have a three-minute glass sand timer so that I wouldn't go overtime. I just wouldn't give up, and Grandma Payne finally sent me the fifteen bucks."

However, once he had the horse, a new problem emerged–how to pay for its feed and upkeep. That motivated the youngster to begin a twelve-mile paper route for the *Roswell Daily Record.* But rather than using a bicycle like the other boys, Norman Brinker delivered his papers on a horse named Silver. And when people saw him ride by, they would yell: "There goes the Lone Ranger."

For the next five years, this first serious job would fund a series of young entrepreneurial pursuits. After a few months, Norman took some of the money he had earned from the paper route and purchased thirteen rabbits for six dollars from one of his customers. His initial idea was to sell them as pets. But their numbers started exploding, and before long he had 150 rabbits. The little boy would go to bed at night and wonder: "Oh, my God! What's it going to look like in the morning." Often he'd wake up to find another six or seven bunnies.

And Norman quickly found out something he never knew about rabbits: "They'd eat through anything that wasn't metal," he remembered, "including the wood that made up my small hutches. Then they would escape and cause another problem. Our neighbors became very unhappy when the rabbits got out and ate their vegetables and plants."

For about a year, all the money he earned from the paper route was either going for food or for building hutches for "those darned rabbits." So, he finally went to his father and said: "Dad, what are we gonna do?" And Gene Brinker looked at his son and said: "Little Boy, you have to learn to take care of yourself. You got into it, you get out of it."

Norman thought about it and decided to have a going-out-of-business sale. And for a kid of eleven, that was a fairly traumatic event. He sold all his bunnies and the hutches for a song. Yet, however painful, Norman treated it as a learning experience. More than fifty years later, he would cite the three basic lessons he had learned: "Begin with the end in mind; sales must equal production; and know how you're going to get *out* before you get *in.*"

Not long after the demise of the rabbit venture, Norman's Aunt Margey came to live with the Brinkers. She brought with her two cocker spaniels and encouraged her nephew, still stung by his failure, to begin raising dogs.

"They don't multiply as fast as rabbits," she assured Norman.

Well, that sounded pretty good, so he once again (at the age of twelve) invested his money and founded what he called Berrendo Kennels (named after the area in which he lived). Immediately, he and his father built fences and housing for the dogs out back where rabbit hutches had once stood. They also constructed some individual dog runs by the family's small orchard–and just like that, Norman Brinker was in the dog business–breeding, selling, training, and showing.

Slowly but surely, the venture grew into a solid market. He had wonderful customers at Walker Air Force Base, where many of the officers would buy puppies. As a matter of fact, Norman was doing such a bang-up business that he was invited to become a charter member of the Roswell Kennel Club.

But then World War II ended, and all the young entrepreneur's customers disappeared. "So, by the time I was fourteen years old," Norman recalled, "I had experienced two traumatic going-out-of-business sales. It was a little easier the second time around, however, and after I lost the cocker spaniels, I would always be thinking about expanding my customer base."

Meanwhile, the paper route was still going. Between the route, working at irrigating cotton and alfalfa fields for five dollars a day, and two entrepreneurial efforts in the animal business–Norman had accumulated $1,300 in his bank account. "My parents were astounded," he said, "not only at the extent of my savings–but that I was also contributing monthly to the family's support. Essentially, I was self-sufficient–and I never again took another penny from my parents for anything, including college."

∼

BEFORE THE WAR STARTED, newspapers were delivered by automobile. But now, due to the shortage of gasoline, the major rural route in the Roswell area was divided into ten or fifteen smaller routes—and one of those belonged to Norman. When the war ended, however, the larger route was restored, and he lost that job as well.

"Undeterred," remembered Norman, "I took three hundred dollars from my savings and purchased fourteen horses (no more unlucky thirteen). And in the same place we had built the rabbit hutches and dog kennels, Dad and I constructed several horse corrals that soon overlapped into the back five acres. At that point, I was in a new business—one that I'd run successfully until I graduated from high school in 1949: Breaking, training, selling, showing—and doing some serious horse trading. Actually, I enjoyed the haggling and the horse trading more than I enjoyed the outcome—even though I usually fared well."

But a single enterprise never seemed to be enough for the energetic young Norman Brinker, who always seemed to be waiting to pounce upon a new opportunity. Well, one sunny afternoon when he was a sophomore in high school, a curious thing happened. Norman had been hurt while breaking a horse—so he took the day off from school and stayed at home to recover. Right after lunch, the gentleman who delivered the *Roswell Daily Record* came by to collect his monthly payment.

"It was a time of day I would not normally have been at home," said Norman. "But I took advantage of the situation to talk to the fellow. I knew that, before the war, the larger paper route was a lucrative job with which people had been able to support their families. So, after paying the monthly bill, I said: 'Say, if you ever, ever want to stop delivering, I would sure like you to consider me to take over the route.' And the response came quickly: 'Well, as a matter of fact,' he said, 'I'm going to stop because I want to get into the ministry—and I want to do it right away.'"

Wasting no time, Norman immediately rode Silver down to the newspaper office and told the circulation manager,

Mr. Bob Beck, that he wanted the job. "At first I was told it was for adults only, because it was a full-time job and extremely important to the paper. But I wouldn't take no for an answer. I reminded Mr. Beck that I had delivered part of the route for four years during the war and never missed a day. 'And this is no more time-consuming than my old paper route–my horse route,' I said. Because of the time pressure to find someone–and the fact that Beck personally liked me, I was finally given the job.

"But there was only one catch that I had not told them," recalled Norman. "I just turned sixteen and had to go out and get a driver's license. The next day, I took three hundred and fifteen dollars from my savings and purchased a car–and then went downtown and passed my driver's test."

At that point, the "Lone Ranger" was delivering newspapers in a 1932 Model A Ford–and was given the title "rural circulation manager" for the *Roswell Daily Record*. "It was a six-day route–one hundred and ten miles long on gravel roads," he remembered. "On weekdays, I got out of school about four, picked up and delivered my papers and returned home between eight and eight thirty. For Sunday deliveries, I left at midnight on Saturday, picked up the papers in Roswell and delivered them so that my customers had their papers by dawn."

In short order, Norm Brinker gained a solid reputation as an honest businessman who provided excellent service. And the route grew in substance because new customers were invariably attracted to his style. Now he would have money enough to support his real passion in life–which was anything to do with horses. That included competing in rodeos, riding in local races, and keeping his business going. From that point on, Norman Brinker's business efforts and his love for horses would be forever linked.

∽

ONE DAY, in early August 1948, as he was delivering papers, Norman noticed a loose horse with a saddle and bridle on the Brinkers' back property. Usually he'd just throw the paper up to the house and keep driving, but this horse piqued his curiosity.

"I stopped the Model A and caught the horse," he said. "I mounted it and was immediately bucked off. Having hung on to the bridle, I got on again and was just as quickly bucked off again. This presented a challenge to me, because, at the time, I considered myself a pretty good horseman—a bareback bronco rider who wasn't used to letting a horse get the best of me. So I got on the mare for a third try, and this time rode her."

"As she eased up a bit, I looked down the road and noticed someone walking my way. Sure enough, the man said that the horse had thrown him off and had run away. Because he was unwilling to handle the horse, he asked if I would be willing to ride her home—which I was pleased to do."

For the next few days, Norman couldn't stop thinking about that horse. He was intrigued by its spirit, and the fact that it was really a beautiful mare. So he went to the owner, Bob Anderson, and bought her for seventy-five dollars.

The horse's name was Loulee, and Norman noticed that she had an "S" brand on her jaw. He rode her down to Roswell's New Mexico Military Institute (which formerly was a cavalry school) to see one of the equestrian experts. "Say," inquired Norman, "can you tell me a little about this horse?"

"Sure," was the response. "Hmmm. Lazy-S brand. That's the mother of Injun Joe."

"Who the hell is Injun Joe?" asked Norman in wonderment.

"Well, he's the famous jumping horse that's been winning everything on the East Coast lately," the man said.

Something clicked in Norman's head. Just a few days before, he had seen a newsreel reporting results of the equestrian jumping competition at the 1948 Olympics. He figured that if Injun Joe could jump, so could his mother Loulee.

Norman asked the man if he could use the jumps at the school to test her out. "Yeah, go ahead," came the friendly response. "Let's see what she can do." Sure enough, Loulee took all the jumps–starting out rough and hesitantly at first. But in a short time, she and Norman rode in harmony as they glided around the course.

"Now, *here* was an opportunity to seize," thought Norm Brinker. "It was one in a million that I had bought Injun Joe's mother. Never would I have been able to afford a jumping horse of this caliber. It was at that point I made the decision to enter the world of competitive jumping–one that would eventually lead me to the 1952 Olympics."

A few days later, he took his parents up to the institute to demonstrate how well he could jump on Loulee. Wanting to show off a little bit, he raised the bars up to four and a half feet. On one of the last jumps, the horse hesitated and threw Norman off–kicking out at the same time and tearing his shirt in the process. The fall scared his mother to death. "Well, that certainly looks dangerous to me," said Kathryn. And Gene Brinker, in his wisdom, simply said: "Little Boy, you've got to learn to ride better than that!"

And for the next two years, Norman took his dad's words to heart. "I strategically set out to become a highly competitive rider," he remembered. "I sought out people who could help me, and, early on, I met a woman named Suzanne Norton, whose father had been a cavalry officer and horse trainer. People around Roswell knew that she was a wizard with horses. Suzanne took me under her wing, trained me, got me started in horse jumping contests–and didn't charge a penny for her time."

Upon graduating from high school, Norman paid his own way through his freshman year at the New Mexico Military Institute (NMMI). He continued to work with Suzanne until she introduced him to a former cavalry jumping instructor. Chink Owens had previously worked with the army's cavalry jumping team—which, up until 1948, had always represented the United States in the Olympic equestrian event. "If you'll do what I tell you to do," Chink told Norman, "and if you'll work as hard as I'll work you, I think you'll have a chance of making the team."

With that kind of a goal, Norman decided to postpone his college sophomore year in an effort to concentrate totally on improving his equestrian skills while Owens worked with his new protégé. "One of our first drills," said Norm, "involved me sitting on a hunt seat—while leaning forward and not touching the horse in any way, except holding the reins. With me in that position, Chink would hold a rope and canter the horse in a circle for twenty-five or thirty minutes. I wasn't allowed to sit down or stand up. I had to hold my arms and legs extended to build my balance and my muscles. It was a brutal drill, but it paid off in the long run."

After a year of hard training and competing in horse shows around the country, Norman set out to win a berth on the United States International Jumping Team—a stepping-stone to his ultimate goal, the Olympics. He finished first in the two regional tryouts held in Santa Fe, New Mexico, and Austin, Texas. Norman then borrowed a horse trailer and made the long drive by himself up to Indiantown Gap, Indiana, for the finals—where he ultimately won a berth after some fierce competition.

With the International Jumping Team, Norman competed in Harrisburg, Pennsylvania, New York's Madison Square Garden, and Toronto, Canada. His parents couldn't have been more proud—and he couldn't have been happier. But when he went to reenroll at NMMI for his sophomore year, the Korean War was on—and Norman had to either get into college, be drafted, or join another branch of the armed forces. Several of his high school friends had either been killed or maimed after being drafted. The ones who survived told him how rough it had been, so he decided the army was not an option.

Right away, Norman went to speak with the man in charge of enrollment at the college—one Colonel Lusk. "Brinker," he said, "I'm on the draft board. So I'll call down and see what your status is. I can't tell you exactly when you're going to be drafted, but I will tell you whether you've got enough time to get your grades up so that you can secure a deferment."

After a quick phone call, the colonel said: "Nope, you don't have time."

And Norman said: "Colonel Lusk, I need two months in order to get ready."

"Brinker," returned the colonel, "I can't tell you when you're going to be drafted, but you don't have two months."

"Well, Colonel Lusk, a month would push me no end to get ready," he replied.

"Brinker, I can't tell you when you're going to be drafted, but you don't have a month."

"Colonel Lusk," said Norman in desperation, "if I just turned my horses out, gave all my stuff away, gave my car away, and quit my paper route—it would take me at least a week to do it."

"Norman, my boy," said the colonel, putting his hand on the young man's shoulder, "I can't tell you exactly when you're going to be drafted, but you don't have a week."

That was enough for Norman. He left the college up on the hill and immediately ran down to the air force recruitment office and tried to enlist. He told the recruiter that he wanted to be headed out of town fast—"day after tomorrow," he said. They administered some tests and told him to return the following day at noon for formal induction. But as he was standing in the recruitment office, the phone rang. "Not one more?" said the recruiter. "I've got one who really looks good, and he's standing right here." When he hung up, the fellow looked at Norman and said: "Sorry, son, they've just closed enlistments."

Instantly, Norman dashed out the door, ran up the stairs, across the lobby, and down the stairs to the navy's recruitment office. The moment he saw their recruiter, he launched into his sales pitch: "My grandfather was in the navy, my father was in the navy, I've got to be in the navy right now." When they asked him to come back later, he insisted on taking the tests right then. They relented, Norm passed, and he was told to return the next day ready to go to San Diego.

When Norman got home and informed his parents what had happened, Kathryn began to cry at the thought of his leaving home for good on such short notice. Gene Brinker, too, was stunned and saddened. He realized that their only son was walking out the door the next day, probably for good. But with a reassuring tone in his voice, he walked over to Kathryn and held her in his arms: "Oh, the little boy will make out all right," he said.

After leaving his folks with instructions on what to do with his possessions, Norman headed out the next day by bus to Albuquerque and then by train to San Diego. The day after that, his draft notice arrived at the Brinkers' house. The young man had always wanted to control his own destiny, and, for him, that meant not being in the army. So it was to be the navy–which turned out to be what he would later call another one of his "lucky breaks."

⁓

WHEN NORMAN ARRIVED at San Diego's Naval Training Base, he thought his chances for going to the Olympics had been completely quashed, and he would be headed for sea duty after finishing boot camp. But then another series of fortunate events occurred.

He met a gentleman named Doc Greenley, who ran the base's laundry and dry-cleaning stores—both civilian enterprises. "Are you the Norman Brinker who's on the International Jumping Team?" inquired Greenley. When the answer came back "yes," Doc Greenley responded: "Well, I read in the *Horse Chronicle* that you were in the navy, so I just waited for your name to come up. When you have time this week, I would like to have you meet some of my friends who show horses. And if you don't have to go to sea, and can stay in San Diego, I will invite you to bring your horse to San Diego and live out here for free."

Then Seaman Third Class Brinker set a goal to continue his quest in making the Olympic Equestrian Team—and he doggedly embarked on a mission to achieve that goal. At first, he did what was expected—he approached his direct superior and asked for permission. "Young man," responded the chief, "you're in the navy now. If they want you, they'll call you. That's lesson number one. Number two is that the navy has no interest in having a horseman around."

Unfazed after that rejection, and being certain that no word leaked back to his direct superior, Norman searched everywhere to find someone with "a more positive and understanding attitude." He went to the base chaplain and asked for help. But there was nothing he could do. He walked over to the Welfare and Recreation Department. No dice. He went to the Athletic Department and was told by people there that they couldn't help unless he was either a football or a basketball player.

Finally, Norman met a lieutenant named Rogansack at the personnel office. "You know, Brinker," he said, "it's the navy's policy to let people who are candidates for the Olympic Team compete. Tell you what. You bring your horse back after boot leave, and I'll have a job for you someplace around here."

And so, when almost all the other recruits were being assigned ship duty on the *U.S.S. Theodore Chandler*, Norman Brinker was given a job as a journalist at the navy's athletic department in San Diego—where he was allowed to spend afternoon hours in training.

In October 1951, Norman Brinker, age twenty, was invited to Fort Riley, Kansas, for the final Olympic qualifying trials. There he became the first navy man ever selected for the United States Equestrian Team. Seven months later, Norman traveled to Helsinki, Finland, for the 1952 Summer Olympics. But because he was by far the youngest member of the team, he was designated as an alternate.

After returning from Helsinki, Norman was given a job as a journalist at the navy's Public Information Office (PIO) in San Diego. He was encouraged to pursue his equestrian career at various shows and competitions in the region.

However, the officer in charge of the PIO, Commander Rowland, was not inclined to let Norman pursue these horse activities. Norman believed Rowland was annoyed by the young sailor's relationship with senior officers.

For example, Norman had asked Rowland for permission to attend one of the largest horse shows in Del Mar, California, about thirty miles away. He had paid the six-hundred-dollar entry fee at a time when he was making only $110 a month as a third class petty officer—a significant investment.

Rowland responded that he needed a formal written request each time Brinker wanted to leave early from the office. So Norman wrote out each request and put them in a mail basket on Rowland's desk. On the first day of the show, the commander delayed Norman's departure by giving him extra work to do. On the last day of the horse show, Norman was waiting anxiously for Rowland to pick up the request from the basket so he could leave on time. But as Commander Rowland reached in that direction, he looked up at the clock and then over at Norman, who knew if he didn't leave right then, he'd miss the most important events of the horse competition and lose most of his entry fee.

With a glare in his eyes, Rowland tossed a stack of mail on top of the request. And Norman knew that was it—he'd never make it now. So, in a fit of rage, Norm picked up his new Smith-Corona typewriter, walked over to the commander's wood and glass enclosed office and threw the machine through the window toward Rowland—causing glass to shatter and fly in every direction.

But rather than throw Brinker in the brig, the commander confined Norman to the upstairs radio room. While Rowland was angry, he wasn't stupid. He apparently was not about to incur the wrath of his superiors should the story get out that he kept Norman from a major competition.

Still rankled, however, Norman looked in the telephone directory, and early one morning called Admiral Martin, commander of the Air Pacific Fleet at his home. Martin set up an appointment later that day, and when Norman arrived, the admiral's fleet secretary called Commander Rowland to find out "what Brinker was up to."

"Why, he isn't up to anything," responded Rowland. "He's confined to the radio room."

"Nope," said the secretary, "he just walked in to see the admiral."

"To see the admiral! To see the admiral!" exclaimed Rowland in shock and disbelief.

Admiral Martin owned a couple of Arabian stallions and really had a great interest in horses. When Norm went in and sat down, he simply asked if the admiral wanted him to participate in the horse shows. "Yes sir," he replied, "that's why you're here. You have a full-time job at the Public Information Office with flexible hours that should work well."

Norman left the admiral's office satisfied that the navy was still encouraging him to ride. But later, when Norm returned to his workstation, Commander Rowland gave him a lengthy drubbing: "If you keep doing things like that, you're going to go to the brig! Do you understand? Young man," he continued, "I confine you to the radio room and you *still* go out and defy me. The problem with you, Brinker, is that you associate with too many officers–and you don't do what you're told. I'm getting rid of you as soon as I can. You're going to be out of here."

At that moment, Norman thought back to the time his mother confined him to the sack for running off–just like Rowland had confined him to the radio room. But Kathryn was worried about his safety. This man, as far as Norman was concerned, was just being mean. But Norman was determined to get back at him in some small way.

"As the designated gopher," recalled Norman, "I would always serve the coffee whenever officers or dignitaries visited the Public Information Office. I also had clean-up duty–so I'd throw several of the coffee cups into the john and flush repeatedly. Then I was always sure to give Commander Rowland one of the cups that came out of the toilet."

∽

DESPITE HAVING A TOUGH TIME with his boss, Norman's personal time in San Diego turned out to contain one of his "lucky breaks." While there, Norman met tennis champion Maureen Connolly. She had just won her first Wimbledon championship, and the city of San Diego, her hometown, wanted to present her with a car. But "Little Mo" said she would rather have a horse–which city officials were happy to provide. And by sheer coincidence, she boarded that horse, Colonel Merry Boy, in the same area Norman kept his horse.

Maureen was a vivacious seventeen-year-old and was writing a sports column for the *San Diego Union.* When she heard Norman Brinker was back from the Olympics, she approached him as he was training and asked if she could interview him for her next column. Norm accepted, and Maureen invited him to her house to have the interview over dinner.

There was an instant attraction between them. And one could easily see that they had more than a few things in common: Both had a passionate love for horses—and both were unusually energetic and athletic.

"I was playing quite a bit of tennis at that time, and thought I was fairly good," recalled Norman. "Also, I had never seen her play, so after the interview, I asked her for a tennis match which, a few nights later, turned out to be our first date.

"Well, Maureen did not ease up on me at all. She'd use a drop shot, a lob, and then she'd smash one by me. Actually, she ran me all over the court. We had been playing about thirty minutes when I walked over to pick up a ball by the fence. Because the lights were shining brightly we couldn't see out—and when I got to the fence, I noticed there were about fifteen people watching us. One kid had his fingers through the fence, and, as I leaned over to pick up the ball, he said: 'Boy, Mister, do we feel sorry for you.'

"After the match, I thought to myself: 'Boy, she is sure some athlete.' And even though I had been thoroughly beaten, I was exhilarated and determined to do better. But the fact is, I never did beat her playing tennis—never even came close."

The couple dated off and on for about a year and became engaged in 1953. Before getting married, however, Norman felt he had to complete his contract with the navy.

Commander Rowland saw to it that he left for sea duty in Japan, where he expected to spend the final eighteen months of his hitch in the navy. But, for reasons Norman never knew, he was transferred to Hawaii in December 1953. While at Pearl Harbor, Norman read a navy publication about the Modern Pentathlon championships that were to be held in Budapest, Hungary, in 1954. Tryouts were just starting, and Norman thought he might be good at the event because, in addition to fencing, it involved horse jumping, swimming, shooting, and running (all of which he had previously done competitively). Besides, he was a bit bored now that his Olympic quest was over. He needed something to set his sights on, so he decided to compete. And to Norm Brinker, exciting competition was like a battery charger.

The first thing he did was to ask his commanding officer to be allowed to participate in the tryouts. Almost instantly a note came back: "If you want to exercise, do sit-ups."

But, as usual, Norman didn't take "no" for an answer. He learned that the liaison to the Olympic athletes in Helsinki, Commander Gutting, was aboard a destroyer that had just arrived for a few days in Pearl Harbor. Timing was once again a factor as Norman was scheduled to ship out to Japan in three weeks. Norman reached him on the phone and simply said: "Commander, I've got a problem. I'd like to try out for the modern pentathlon, but my commanding officer has other plans for me. Can you help?"

"Norman," responded Commander Gutting, "you know if I had all the pull in the world I wouldn't be on this damned destroyer. But I think I've got enough pull that I can take care of your problem. Let me see what I can do."

Two days later, Commander Gutting strolled into the office of Norman's boss and stayed about thirty minutes. Upon walking out, he gave Norman the thumbs-up sign. Less than a week later, Petty Officer Brinker was given a permanent assignment as a journalist for the Fifth Naval District, which would allow him once again to start the quest to compete in the Modern Pentathlon world championship competition in Budapest, Hungary.

The Modern Pentathlon consisted of five athletic events held over a five-day period. The first day was a cross-country equestrian event three miles long with twenty-eight jumps. The second day involved fencing with a dueling point sword. The third event was pistol shooting—twenty shots at a revolving target. On the fourth day, the athletes swam four hundred meters; and the last event was a three-mile cross-country run.

At night, Norman would write up the navy's softball games and other athletic events. But his days were free to practice running, swimming, and shooting with numerous other navy athletes who were hoping to land a berth for the All-Navy Triathlon competition in San Diego—which was the first step to Budapest (where riding and fencing would be included).

Within a few months, important decisions had to be made as to which men would be allowed to compete. The officers who were to make those decisions held a conference in a room right next to Norman's desk—where he listened with intense concentration. A number of athletes were quickly dropped. "Smith, no way. Johnson, gone. Jones, out." And then they got to Brinker, whom, curiously, they referred to by his first name. "What about Norman," one of them finally said. "Well, he's fine in the shooting and running. But his swimming is about three seconds off. Oh, what the hell. He's been working very hard and improving all the time. We ought to let him go. Yeah, let's let Norman go."

So Norman Brinker proceeded to San Diego to compete in the All-Navy games—in which he won a gold medal. He then moved on to Camp Lejune, North Carolina, for the interservice competition where he qualified for the final team. In addition to Norman, three other American athletes were selected for the world championships. But only three of them were going to be allowed to compete—one would be an alternate. This time, Norman was determined to be one of the regulars. But it was going to be an uphill battle. Not only was he, at twenty-two, the youngest of the four to try out—two of the other three athletes had competed in the last Olympics or the most recent Pan Am Games—and the third had set a national swimming record at the University of Colorado. Moreover, they took it for granted that "the little guy," as they called him, was definitely going to be the benchwarmer.

The team left for Europe about six weeks early to get in some fencing practice in Germany. And Norman, as usual, made good use of the time. He knew that his weak point was swimming. If he didn't improve his time by several seconds, he thought, he'd surely be relegated to alternate status.

So, while in Berlin, he sought out a famous German swimming coach who trained in the area. "I've got a problem," Norman told the coach. "I don't make a lot of money—only seventy-five dollars a month. But, I'll tell you what I'll do. I'll give you one hundred dollars if you can knock fifteen seconds off my time in the four-hundred-meter freestyle.

"There are only two provisos," he went on. "*First*, I can practice anytime in the morning before seven, or after eight at night, and *second*, nobody—but **nobody**—on the American team must know anything about this. What do you say, coach?"

Norman knew the German got the message when he boomed back in broken English: "Ach! Get in! Swim! Kick one hundred meters!"

So Norman kicked one hundred meters.

"Ach! Pull the one hundred meters!" said the coach.

So he pulled one hundred meters.

"Ach!" yelled the German. "Strong! Strong! But stiff, stiff! We'll work! Work! Work! Work!"

"Can you knock fifteen seconds off?" asked Norman hopefully.

"Ach, I can knock more than that off! You're *stiff!*" he boomed, "but with a lot of work we can make big improvements!"

"Yeah, okay," said Norman. "Work we will."

For six weeks leading up to the final trials, Norman secretly worked with the German swimming coach. Then came the day of the tryout that would make so much difference. Norman had registered some good scores in the other four events, and everyone knew swimming would decide who the alternate would be.

For the race, Norman was lined up beside his teammate, Bill Andre, who would routinely beat Norm by four or five lengths in the four hundred meters. At the two-hundred-meter mark, they were dead even. At three hundred meters, Norman was leading by about two lengths. For those last one hundred meters, Norman really put his head down and powered it home. When he touched the wall and looked up, he had beaten his teammate by a full four lengths. The American coach and the other athletes were astounded. Norman was in. He had earned a starting spot and could not be denied.

A DAY BEFORE THE COMPETITION began in Budapest, the four American athletes walked the equestrian course with some local horsemen. Norman struck up a friendly conversation with the designer of the course, and they strategically discussed the twenty-eight jumps and how each should be approached.

Jumps twenty-four and twenty-five, in particular, attracted Norman's attention. At that point, the horses jumped a fence onto a bridge, and immediately came up to a huge tree everyone planned to go around. The next jump involved a set of logs with some scattered tree stumps on the far side. Most riders went around the tree so that they could negotiate the next jump straight on.

Well, Norman decided to jump the bridge at an angle, duck down, go under the tree, and come in at an angle to the jump near the big logs. He figured that, all told, he could save three seconds doing it that way—even though it was risky.

The next day, the world championship competition began with the horse jumping event. There were about sixty people representing twenty countries. Every three minutes an individual rider began the three-mile run. Norman took off near the end of the grouping and was flying around the course at record speed as spectators cheered him on and yelled that he was in the lead. Then he came up to jumps twenty-four and twenty-five. He took the jump onto the bridge in good shape, but a branch on the tree snagged him, and slightly disrupted the horse's gait and timing. The stallion then started the next jump one stride too soon. The horse fell as he hit the log—and catapulted Norman out of the saddle. He hit hard on his left shoulder, heard a definite crack, and then felt excruciating pain. But he held on to the reins, got back on his mount, negotiated the last three jumps, and finished the race.

As soon as he ended the run, Norman informed officials that he had broken his shoulder. What he didn't know at the time was that he had actually suffered a broken collarbone near the joint of his left shoulder. Despite the fall, Norm Brinker placed eighth in the field of sixty.

He was immediately whisked off to the local hospital, where doctors were unable to set his collarbone because of the location of the break. So they immobilized his left arm by extending it outward, bending it at the elbow, and putting it in a metal sling. He was then given some pills for the pain and placed in a room for a few days to recover.

At this time, in 1954, at the height of the Cold War, there were only about twenty-five Americans in the country. Later that evening, Norman's hospital room became jam-packed with Hungarians who were interested not only in him but also in any news from America. They devoured all the magazines that the American consul had sent over–and they bombarded him with questions. "Is it true that Jesse Owens is now shining shoes in the streets of New York? That's what we've been told." Norman answered that it was *not* true. Jesse was an insurance executive.

"How about Lauren Bacall," they inquired. "How are she and Humphrey Bogart doing?" He didn't have an answer for that one.

Finally, all the lingering Hungarians left his room. And Norm took some time to reflect on what had just happened. Two thoughts crossed his mind:

The attention he had garnered, combined with the astounding propaganda that communism had inflicted on the people of Hungary, deeply affected Norman. He knew then, more than ever, that the United States of America was the best place on earth to live. And, after all the rodeos, all the riding, and all the spills he had endured up until that point, Norman had never been seriously injured. This was the first major horse accident he had ever experienced–and it happened at the worst possible time. Being unable to compete in the last four events of the Modern Pentathlon was a very hard thing for him to accept.

As he lay alone in his hospital bed, unable to move his left arm and shoulder, Norman Brinker wondered how long he would be stuck there. And, as thoughts of what "might have been" raced through his mind, he closed his eyes and gently drifted into a deep sleep.

BRINKER PRINCIPLES

....

- Begin with the end in mind.
- When you see a wrong, right it. Get involved personally.
- It is never acceptable to be doing things only for yourself.
- You should be a well-rounded individual—dedicated to family, business, and community.
- If you say you're going to do something, you must follow through.
- Never, ever tell anything but the truth.
- You are responsible for your own actions.
- Set goals and be persistent in achieving your dreams. Don't take "no" for an answer. Never, never give up.
- Learn from your failures—and move on.
- Always be thinking about expanding your customer base.
- If you simply tell people you have a problem, you'll be amazed at how much they'll want to help you.
- Let your natural curiosity lead you forward.
- Seek out coaches who have expertise in what you want to achieve. Listen and learn.
- Seize every potential opportunity.

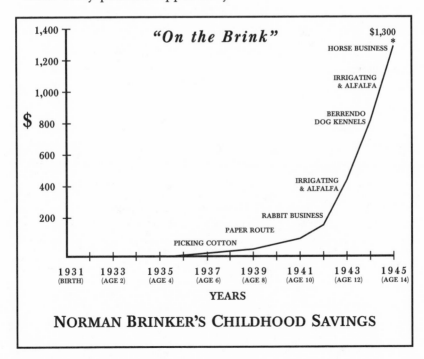

NORMAN BRINKER'S CHILDHOOD SAVINGS

3

*"We want to be very honest with you.
Quite frankly, Mr. Brinker's injury is very,
very serious. It's possible he may live only
four to six days."*

ONE OF FIVE ATTENDING PHYSICIANS,
to Nancy Brinker

*"I know Norman. He's my patient. I have
a feeling he's going to be okay. I'm not
ready to give him up."*

DR. PHIL WILLIAMS,
to the Brinker family

*"There's a lot left that I want to do. But
I'm not afraid of dying."*

NORMAN BRINKER
to daughter, Brenda, when she was a teenager

The Diagnosis

N ancy could hear the phone ringing at the nurse's station in the Intensive Care Unit just outside Norman's room. She was informed that it was the Brinker's friend, Ross Perot, calling from Dallas. He had just heard about the accident on the radio.

"How is he, Nancy?" asked Perot.

"Oh, Ross," she sighed, "I'm looking at him right now through the window. He hasn't moved at all since we got him here a few hours ago. They've got all these tubes hooked up to him. It just doesn't look very good."

"What do you need?" Ross asked Nancy.

"Well, I'd like Norman to have the very best medical care we can possibly get. I also think we need Phil Williams down here right away."

"Do we need to move Norm? Is it safe to move him?"

"I don't know yet, Ross," she replied.

"Nancy, don't worry about a thing. I'll take care of it. I'll call you back in a few minutes."

With that, Perot quickly phoned the president of Southwestern Medical Center in Dallas for advice. He knew that Southwestern had four Nobel Prize winners on staff and that it was one of the best health-care facilities in the world. Several experts were recommended to work with the doctors in Florida–including a trauma specialist and, as Nancy requested, Dr. Phil Williams, who also insisted on bringing in two specialists to ensure that the CAT (Computerized Axial Tomography) scans were technically sound and perfectly interpreted.

Dr. Williams, one of the leading neurosurgeons in Dallas, immediately dropped everything, organized the trip, and raced to the airport. This was more than another mission to save a life, he thought. It involved Norm Brinker, a man he admired, respected, and considered a dear friend. Ross was touched by Dr. Williams' immediate response.

By nightfall, all the doctors had been contacted, preparations made, and Ross Perot's private plane mobilized for the flight to Florida. The Dallas medical team arrived to join the physicians at St. Mary's on Friday afternoon—within twenty-four hours of the accident.

Meanwhile, Nancy was busy contacting family and friends. She called daughters Brenda, who flew in from Maryland, and Cindy, who hopped a jet from Dallas. Son Eric flew in from Boston. Nancy's parents, Ellie and Marvin Goodman, drove the one hundred miles from their home in Ft. Lauderdale. And Mr. and Mrs. Max Fisher and Mr. and Mrs. Vince Paul, the Brinkers' close friends from Palm Beach, rushed right over to the hospital.

At the same time, Dr. Sandy Carden helped Nancy assemble the team of local physicians who would immediately attend Norman. They included a couple of seasoned neurosurgeons and an outstanding critical-care specialist. They examined Norman extensively before the team from Dallas arrived—and Nancy was there for every early examination and test. She wanted to be certain her husband was receiving the best care possible—and she wanted to know exactly *what* was going on *when* it was going on.

After their first thorough analysis, one of the Florida doctors came out and spoke to Nancy: "We want to be very honest with you," said one sternly. "Quite frankly, Mr.

Brinker's injury is very, very serious. It's possible he may live only four to six days."

By the time the other physicians arrived from Dallas, Nancy was understandably upset and nervous. She had not heard very much good news.

Upon his arrival, Dr. Williams went directly to see Nancy. "Are you all right?" he inquired.

"Oh, Phil," she replied, "the doctors here don't think he's going to make it."

"Nancy, you and I both know that if anyone can pull out of this, it's Norman," he said reassuringly. "Now, tell me exactly what happened on the polo field."

After hearing the details of the accident, Dr. Williams joined the other physicians to review CAT scans, X rays, and other data. All afternoon, there was a steady flow of medical personnel going in and out of Norman's room in the ICU.

Dr. Williams was the last of the medical team members to conduct a full examination. He found Norman Brinker to be profoundly unconscious and intubated (on a mechanical respirator). One of the first things he noticed was that only one-half of Norman's body sweated. His left forehead, for example, was perspiring profusely—but the other side was completely dry. The doctor then checked the patient's reflexes and spoke to him—but there was absolutely no response to stimulus. He looked at the pupils of Norman's eyes, but they were so small he could not ascertain whether there was swelling in the optic nerve.

Dr. Williams also checked for common reflex reactions. He rubbed Norman's chest looking for signs of inward limb movement—technically referred to as decerebrate rigidity. What he observed was not encouraging. Norman had significant inward movement on his left side but only partial motion on the right. The doctor then rubbed the bottom of Norman's left foot and noted an upgoing big toe.

He was heard to utter a muffled "Uh, oh," as he recorded a positive Babinski—another diagnostic sign indicative of cranial trauma.

It was from these critical observations, reasoned Dr. Williams, that the other doctors were offering little hope to Nancy. After all, most comatose patients who display such symptoms usually die within seventy-two hours of the time the injury was sustained.

Upon completion of his examination, Dr. Williams told Nancy that it was, indeed, a very grave injury. "But, if Norman can survive for the next two to three days," said the physician, "he has a good chance to make it." At that point, the two held hands right outside the ICU and said a prayer together for Norman. "We'll need the Lord's help on this one," thought Dr. Williams.

∼

ON MONDAY AFTERNOON, following a solemn weekend, all the doctors gathered to evaluate Norman's condition—which had not changed at all. He had now been in a coma for ninety-six hours, and the only positive sign they could muster up was that he was still alive.

After agreeing that all the key information was now in, the medical team called for a late-night conference with the family to review the test results. Nancy Brinker, her parents Ellie and Marvin Goodman, Eric, Brenda, the Fishers, the Pauls, and Sandy Carden gathered with the doctors in a hospital meeting room at 10:30 P.M. Each physician evaluated the information independently and objectively—and all agreed on the general diagnosis.

Every scan that was taken showed small pools of blood scattered throughout Norman's head. Dr. Williams officially described it as "a closed-head injury with significant multi-foci cerebral contusion." Essentially, it was bruising on the brain.

"Similar to a bruise under the skin, blood will hemorrhage into the bruised tissues and create a black and blue mark on the skin," Dr. Williams explained. "That is essentially what has happened to Norman, with the highest concentrations in the right parietal area–which directly affects the left side of his body."

The physicians also explained that there were numerous signs that Norman's injuries were particularly grave. "We have noticed several reflexes that indicate his limbs may be turning inward," mentioned one doctor as he referred to the positive Babinski and decerebrate rigidity. "Some people would interpret it as a sign that the body may be preparing for death," he told Nancy.

Finally, the doctors stated that Norman was in a deep coma. "There's a range of scale for comas–from one to ten," they told the family. "A 'one' is the worst–where there is no consciousness at all, and the damage may be permanent. Mr. Brinker is in a number-one coma, and there are signs he may have such damage," said one doctor.

At this point, Eric broke down and ran out of the room in tears, and his grandmother followed him. "Eric, you're not helping your mom any," said Ellie as she held him in her arms. "This is where you have to be strong."

"I can't do it," said Eric.

"Yes, you can do it," she responded. "This is where you have to be tough as nails. This is where you're going to turn into a man. Now, let's go back in there."

All the physicians sat down on one side of the conference table, as if on a panel; family and friends were on the other side. Interestingly enough, while the doctors all agreed on the general diagnosis, there was some difference of opinion on the patient's prognosis. Regarding Norman's chances for recovery, the doctors spoke one at a time–in very serious and stern tones.

"I don't think he's going to make it," predicted one. "Very few people who have decerebrate rigidity survive—very few. They just don't come back. It's a *very bad* sign."

"If he does wake up," said another, "he's basically going to be in a vegetative state. He'll have to be respirated for the rest of his life."

Two other physicians were likewise extremely pessimistic. "There simply is no history of other patients who have suffered these types of injuries undergoing any kind of meaningful recovery."

Dr. Phil Williams spoke last. In calm, soothing tones with a slight emotional tint, he said: "I know Norman. He's my patient. I have a feeling he's going to be okay. I'm not ready to give him up."

Dr. Williams went on to emphasize the intangibles of Norman's determination and physical strength. He pointed out that two months before the accident, Norman had taken his yearly physical. At that time, he was in the 99.6 percentile for physical fitness in his age group. "If Norman can be maintained on life support," said the doctor, "and doesn't have extra effects like massive swelling, or a blood clot, or an infection, or a pulmonary embolism (blocked vein going to the lung)—then he will survive, and hopefully have a functional recovery."

Family and friends on the other side of the table were either crying or in shock. After a long pause, Nancy told the doctors that Norman had a living will. "He made me swear to him, if there's ever a question of living on a life support system or letting him go—he didn't want to stay," she said, her voice choking with emotion. "If you're telling me that he's not going to recover—then we'll make our decision within a few days."

"Nancy," answered Dr. Williams. "We just don't know yet. There's a chance he could recover—but there is also a very high chance that there is going to be no further recovery of cognitive function and no motor function at all on one side."

In spite of the negative diagnosis, Norman's daughter, Brenda, had no doubts that her father was going to recover completely. Her thoughts drifted back several years to a conversation she and her dad had about death. "You know, Brenda," Norman told her, "when I die I want it to be when I'm on a polo pony—when I'm riding and doing something I really love to do."

"Dad," she remembered saying, "you don't want to die, do you?"

"Oh, no, no, no," said Norm. "Don't misunderstand me. I don't want to leave this world. There's a lot left that I really need to do. But, I've been able to accomplish those things that I've wanted to accomplish. I've set meaningful goals, worked toward them, and achieved most of them. All I'm saying to you is that I'm not afraid of dying."

∽

ALL OF THE PHYSICIANS felt very strongly that Norman should be kept right where he was; that St. Mary's was an excellent hospital providing excellent care. They also agreed that there were no surgical options—unless, over a period of days, he developed a blood clot.

The consensus was that there was nothing to do but wait.

Dr. Williams summed it all up in a private whisper to Nancy. "To a very large degree," he said, "Norman is in control of his own destiny. We'll have to see if his body and his subconscious can pull him out and bring him back. It's true, he's got to come back against the odds. If anyone can do it, Norman can. But it's going to be day to day from here on out."

The medical conference broke up quickly. It was quite late, and no one seemed to have anything else to say. Everyone either went home or to their hotel rooms—except Nancy. She went down to intensive care to be with her husband.

4.

"I learned very early to put myself in the
shoes of the customer. I asked myself:
'What kind of cutlery would be of most
benefit to this person?'"

NORMAN BRINKER,
*on putting himself through college selling
cutlery door-to-door*

"Norman, why should I invite you to join
me to help build my dream?"

BOB PETERSON,
*owner of Jack-In-The-Box,
to Norm Brinker during a job interview, 1957*

"Congratulations, Norman. You're now in
charge of Jack-In-The-Box."

BOB PETERSON,
two months after Norm started with Peterson's company

Cutlery and Jack-In-The-Box

A fter the riding accident in Budapest, Norm was transferred stateside to Annapolis, Maryland, to complete the final two months of his hitch in the navy. He used the time not only to let his shoulder mend, but also to contemplate seriously what he was going to do in the next stage of his life.

Norman came to the conclusion that his destiny was clearly in San Diego. He planned to marry Maureen and enroll at San Diego State University to finish college. In addition to really liking California, he believed the state's vigorous economy gave him more options from which to choose once he obtained his degree. There was only one problem with this plan, however: Because his overriding interest was to prepare for the International Jumping Team, Norman's grades had suffered during his freshman year. So it was not a sure thing that he'd be automatically accepted into a new college.

Upon returning to the West Coast, Norm applied for entrance to San Diego State University (SDSU) in person. He went directly to the dean of admissions who, after reviewing the record, related a pessimistic message: "I'm sorry, Norman," said the dean, "your grades just aren't high enough. We suggest you go to junior college."

"That doesn't sound like a good approach," he replied. "I want to come here. My efforts were focused then on making the Olympic Team. Now, my only interest is coming to SDSU and doing very well. I guarantee you that my being here will be an asset—and I'll be an outstanding student."

"Well, we can't take anyone who has less than a 2.5 average. Sorry. The odds of you being accepted are not good at all."

But Norman just would not give up. He persisted until the dean finally said: "Well, there's one way you *can* make it, but I think you're wasting your time. Here's a list of people who are on our admissions committee. You pick out one of these names and go meet that person. Tell the committee member your story, and maybe they'll go to bat for you at our admissions meeting for special cases."

"Fine, thank you," replied Norman as he quickly headed out the door.

Over the next couple of days, Norm made appointments to see all six people on the list. Most members gave him a polite audience but remained noncommittal in regard to support and sponsorship. But when he met Dean Brookshire, the dean of women, she emphasized why the others were lukewarm to his request. "Norman," she said, "we all know about you. We know you have athletic pursuits that require a lot of time. We know you didn't make the grades at NMMI because you were interested in going to the Olympics.

"Gosh," she said, pointing to her window, "if a load of hay comes by here, you might go follow that hay truck to where it's going. I just don't believe you'll commit and stick around!"

"Mrs. Brookshire," responded Norman, "my mother used to have the same problem with me—and so did the navy. But things have changed. When I got out of the Olympics in 1952, I never gave a thought toward competing in 1956. And I've already told officials that I'm not going to the upcoming Pan-Am Games next year to compete in the Modern Pentathlon. I have no interest whatsoever in pursuing an athletic career. That's history—and that's my other life.

"I do have an interest now in getting a college education," he continued. "I'm also going to get married. Please give me a chance. I promise, you'll be very happy that you let me come to school here."

Norman's sincerity seemed to do the trick. A few weeks later, Dean Brookshire persuaded the rest of the admissions committee to make an exception. As a result, he enrolled in the marketing program at San Diego State University. And in making good on his promise to the dean, he graduated with distinction in 1957 after having compiled all A's and only one B in three years of study.

∼

ON JUNE 19, 1955, following completion of his first college semester, Norman married Maureen Catherine Connolly. She had won Wimbledon three times, the U.S. Open three times (the first in 1953 at age sixteen), and the French Open twice. And, in 1953, she was the first woman to win the Grand Slam of Tennis—which included the championships of Australia, France, Great Britain, and the United States. As a matter of fact, in the last two years of her tennis career, she never lost a set in a major tournament. During Maureen's prime, she was the world's third most popular female subject of newspaper and magazine articles (behind Mamie Eisenhower and Madame Nehru)—and she was affectionately known as "America's Sweetheart."

But while Norman had frequently watched her practice tennis, he never saw Maureen play a professional match. For the most part, he was in the navy traveling while she was winning tournaments. And then, tragically, a horse-riding accident cut short her career in 1954 at the age of nineteen. She was hit on the leg by the loose chute of a moving cement truck. The collision not only threw her off the horse, it severed tendons and arteries in her right leg. While she was able to recover enough to become the pro at the Balboa Tennis Club in San Diego, Maureen was never again able to regain her top athletic form or play tournament tennis.

In the years following the accident, she became a journalist for both the *San Diego Union* and the *London Daily Mail.* She also did television work for major tournaments. As a matter of fact, Maureen and Norman went to London on their honeymoon so she could cover the 1955 Wimbledon championships for the *Mail.*

While his new wife made a salary with her professional work, Norman (because he never ceased following his father's advice to take care of himself) insisted on supporting her and paying his own tuition at San Diego State. In the navy, he had supplemented his enlisted pay by taking a part-time job selling cutlery door-to-door.

As a matter of fact, one of the first questions Maureen's mother, Jessemine Connolly, asked Norman was how he intended to support her daughter.

"Well," he responded enthusiastically. "I'm going to sell cutlery door-to-door, just like I did in the navy."

"How can you do that when people are now putting up *No Solicitors* signs in their windows all over the neighborhood?" asked Mrs. Connolly.

"Oh," said Norman quickly, "those are the houses I'm going to first. They'll be more receptive because other salesmen don't badger them."

Actually, Norman enjoyed working on commission, because the harder he worked, the more he was paid. He also liked the flexibility of setting his own hours–which would usually be between 6 and 10 in the evenings.

All in all, it was a perfect way to put himself through college. So Norman went back to the managers of Cutco, a division of Wearever, and asked to be reinstated as a salesman–which, because of past success, was done without hesitation.

Norman essentially worked on reference. He'd ask customers for advice on who might be interested in some of his products. When they'd offer the names of a few friends, he would write down the addresses and then ask if the customer would "call them and tell them that I'm coming." Ninety percent of the time, they'd say "Sure." As a result, many of Norm's customers already knew he was coming when he knocked on the door. After a while, Cutco's in-house magazine, *The Blade,* was carrying regular articles about the success of two young salesmen: Norman Brinker and Irv Deal, who were record-setters for the highest percentage of sales per call (or display). The two also maintained a lifelong friendship and were to become partners in future business dealings many years later.

"I learned very early on," Norman explained, "to put myself in the shoes of the customer. I asked myself: 'What kind of cutlery would this person be interested in?' Then I'd propose, not for them to buy, but: 'What would be the best day for delivery—the first or the fifteenth? Which set would you prefer?' Sometimes people would respond: 'Well, I'm not sure I want to buy.' Then I'd persist by showing different options or ideas, and they'd usually purchase something."

Selling cutlery door-to-door brought in a significant amount of money for the Brinkers. The job not only put Norman through school, its flexibility allowed him the time to pursue other extracurricular interests.

During his junior year, for instance, Norman became involved in a campaign to institute universal activity fees as part of student tuition expenses. All extracurricular activities, including the athletic budget, were paid for from the fund. But because the university was state-sponsored, a two-thirds vote of the student body was necessary to charge the fees on a nonvoluntary basis. Similar proposals had failed several times in the past. This time, though, Norman became one of the leaders of the initiative and held rallies, information forums, and a general campaign of education. The group instituted a slogan to get everybody's curiosity going–and *"Put State on the Map"* was plastered all over campus.

When the measure passed, Norman became known around the university as an active leader. And because he felt it important to see that the money was distributed properly, Norm ran for student body president. After assembling a team of friends and developing a strategy, he campaigned hard–complete with a slogan and with rallies. He also went personally to all the fraternities and sororities on campus in an effort to get to know people. In the end, he won the election by a sizable margin over a very strong fraternity candidate–and became the first nonfraternity student body president in the school's history.

So, in his senior year at San Diego State, Norman carried up to twenty-one hours per semester, held down his cutlery sales job *and* threw himself into his new school responsibilities with typical zest and vigor. And while performing his duties as president, a curious coincidence occurred that Norm would never forget. It was one of those "events" that just seemed to happen when he became involved in things.

He had been thinking about the impact of the 1956 Hungarian Revolution and became concerned about escaping immigrants. So he organized a fund-raising group to sponsor living expenses for three Hungarian students at the university. As they arrived on campus, one of the students immediately walked up to Norman and asked him if he had participated on the United States Pentathlon Team in Budapest three years before.

When Norm confirmed he had, the Hungarian grinned broadly and said: "After your accident, when you came over to the gym to watch the fencing competition, I was the guy who opened the door for you and took you through the crowd. Everybody recognized you with your arm up and immobilized. Remember, they gave you a standing ovation.

Our people admired the fact that you got back on your horse and finished the race. You were a real hero to us."

Norman was astounded. He had never fully realized the high opinion Hungarians had of him after the accident. He thought the crowd felt sorry for him and was just being polite.

The student government experience afforded Norman the opportunity to begin honing his leadership skills. He felt very strongly, for instance, about obtaining large majority support on any major initiative. And he quickly came to realize that the first step in convincing others of the justice of his cause was to listen to *their* views on the issue. "I learned that a leader must motivate people from their own self-interest to accomplish the maximum good," he recalled. "And real leaders must be 100 percent straight and open with their associates."

This philosophy was, in part, the foundation for what Norman would refer to in later years as obtaining a "psychological commitment" from others. Moreover, in the very near future, he would effectively apply these and other lessons in building a successful business career.

NORMAN BEGAN LOOKING FOR a job during his junior year at San Diego State. He knew he would be twenty-six years old when he graduated and felt it important to be thinking ahead. If he interviewed with people early, he reasoned, then they would know him when graduation rolled around. It was also a big advantage for him to see what was available and have the ability to pick and choose his own course rather than being in a desperate situation once college was over.

He interviewed with dozens of companies leading up to his graduation, including Procter & Gamble, Shell Oil, Sears, Bethlehem Steel—all for marketing positions. Often he would receive a job offer at an initial interview. When he went home, Maureen would ask him how it went, and he'd reply: "Well, honey, they offered me a job, but it just didn't sound like fun—so I said, 'Probably not.'" Norman later confessed that, after about a year, Maureen got a little bit impatient (as any wife would) with that particular reason for turning down good jobs.

But Norman later convinced himself that taking his time was the right thing to do. Moreover, going to college a few years later than most people—or getting "a slow start out of the blocks," as he said—wasn't all that bad. "I had done a lot of things in those earlier years that had enabled me to grow as a person," said Norman. "I really felt I had to know life before I could succeed at anything."

Being a bit more mature also aided his ability to concentrate. Frequently he would take a few extra courses just because he was interested. For instance, during Norm's senior year, Henry Nunn, the retired chairman of Nunn-Busch (one of the world's largest shoe manufacturers), taught a class one semester from 6 to 9 P.M. When Norman heard about it, he quickly signed up and revised his selling routine for that one night each week. The course subsequently turned out to have a great impact on his future business philosophy.

Mr. Nunn discussed how his corporation had been doing very well up until the early 1930s. But when the negative backlash of the Great Depression began to take effect, Nunn-Busch started to go broke. So he resolved to do something really different to ensure the corporation's future success.

"We decided to form a partnership with our employees," Mr. Nunn told his students. "We actually gave them a percentage of the business—about 20 percent. When we had to implement cost-cutting measures, we let them decide what to do. Usually the choice was either a reduction in hours or layoffs."

Mr. Nunn went on to explain that discipline problems were handled automatically by their new partners. Tardiness, absenteeism, and lack of performance all but disappeared, because the guy next door took care of it. "In addition," said Mr. Nunn, "we let them decide how fast the line should go. And the most amazing thing happened: The speed of the line picked up 20 percent. And product quality increased, because everyone cared." This one session, which could have been a night selling cutlery (and making some money), became one of the keys to Norman Brinker's evolving business philosophy.

While in college, Norman also obtained some on-the-job marketing experience when he formed an athletic apparel importing business. He and Maureen opened the Balboa Park Tennis Shop, which featured Teddie Tinling designer tennis clothes. Tinling shipped the clothes in from England, and Norman then packed them in smaller quantities, and distributed the apparel to various shops in the San Diego-Los Angeles area.

"It was a small company," Norman explained, "but it looked promising. And it was the line of business I intended to pursue in life—until I met a fellow named Peterson."

Bob Peterson owned the well-known and successful Oscar's Coffee Shops—and a new five-unit chain of fast-food restaurants called Jack-In-The-Box. All the restaurants were in San Diego, and Norman had heard of Peterson because the university's marketing classes used his success story as a local example of multiple operations.

As a result, Norm's curiosity was aroused when a professor one day mentioned to him that Peterson wanted a meeting. The entrepreneur had heard of Norm's work on campus—and also knew of Maureen Connolly.

When Norman went down to Peterson's office for an interview, he never dreamed of being interested in the restaurant business. But, almost immediately, he noticed a difference between this potential job and all the others he had been checking out. First of all, the forty-five-year-old Peterson was surrounded by energetic young people, including a good friend of Norman's, Marvin Braddock, who had graduated from college a year earlier. The youth and vibrancy created an excitement in the air, and he immediately wanted to be a part of it. And, second, Norm found Peterson sitting comfortably on a sofa—dressed in an open-neck, brown checked shirt and a brown pair of slacks. His casual nature, which Norman liked, was in marked contrast to the stiff coats and ties of his more formal interviews with larger companies.

After a greeting, Peterson asked a to-the-point question: "Norman," he said, "why should I invite you to join me to help build my dream?"

"Boy, oh boy," thought Norm, "this guy is really different. He has some direction. He knows where he's going. He has a dynamic dream."

Norman's mind swiftly went into overdrive as he came up with a dozen or more reasons why Peterson should hire him. After the interview, he filled out an employment application in which there was a question that asked: "Why should we consider you for this job?" Norman answered with a brief but positive sentence: "I have the ability to make things happen," he wrote.

After a solid recommendation from Marvin Braddock, Bob Peterson offered Norman a job, and, the day after obtaining his marketing degree, Brinker began his career in the restaurant business—as a *busboy*—complete with a little paper hat. After a week cleaning up dirty dishes, his next job was in the kitchen flipping hamburgers for about a month.

All of the college students ate at the Oscar's near campus where Norm started, and Peterson wanted to see whether the young man could absorb all the flak he would receive from his buddies. And kid him they did. "Hey, Brinker," the guys would yell. "What good was that college education? You could have gotten a job as a fry cook four years ago and saved lots of time and money!"

Norm tried to take all the ribbing good-naturedly and hoped that Peterson would take note of his hard work. But the truth was that Brinker's boss already had plans for him. With a laugh, Peterson would comment twenty years later: "Damn right, I started him out in the basement. But I knew he could take it. I saw potential in him. I saw the spark that kindles success."

A couple of months later, Peterson called Norm down to the main office and informed him that he was sending a number of executives up to Los Angeles to manage a new chain of restaurants–and that there might be a need for a supervisor of Jack-In-The-Box. "Do you think you could handle that job?" asked Peterson.

"Yes, I think so–absolutely!" responded Norman.

"Well, we'll let you know what our decision is," said Peterson. "But first we'd like you to do some training at Jack-In-The-Box. This is Ed Bolling," said Peterson pointing to a fellow who suddenly appeared in the doorway. "Ed, can you take Norman out to your restaurant and train him?"

"I don't want to see the son-of-a-bitch today, tomorrow, or any other time," responded Bolling gruffly.

Norman's thoughts at that moment were: "Well, this guy has some kind of problem. Maybe we could do the training somewhere else,"–which is exactly what happened.

After a week of firsthand experience in a Jack-In-The-Box restaurant, Norm was again called back to see Peterson. As he walked into the office building, people were congratulating him, and he responded with a beaming smile and said "thank you" to everyone. He thought the congratulations were for the birth of his first child, Cindy, just a few days earlier. But, when he got into the boss's office, Peterson said: "Congratulations, Norman. You're now in charge of Jack-In-The-Box."

First, it was down to an automobile dealership for a new '57 Chevrolet–his company car. Then he and Peterson took off to visit all of the Jack-In-The-Box restaurants. During the early going, Bob Peterson counseled Norman to visit people in person and to be sure to include them on his team. "Listen to them, really listen to them," he advised. "Be fair to them, and let them get involved in a meaningful way."

Little did Norman know that almost immediately he would have some difficulty following his boss's advice because of an employee who resented the younger Brinker becoming the new supervisor. A year earlier, Peterson had offered franchises to the managers of Jack-In-The-Box. All but one took it. The lone exception was Ed Bolling, who thought he was going to be the future supervisor. Naturally, he was quite upset when Brinker got the job.

On Norman's first few visits to his restaurant, Bolling was just as hostile as he could be. On the third visit, Norm ventured out just before lunch and was looking at the new microwave (which Peterson believed was going to be a thing of the future) and the sign next to it that listed cooking times for hamburgers, chicken, and shrimp, et cetera–when Bolling suddenly reached up and yanked the sign off the wall and stuck it in his pocket. "Now, we'll see what you can do without the list," he said. "You don't know what the times are. So *now* what are you going to do, Brinker?"

"I'll tell you what I'm going to do," Norman responded angrily. "I'm going to leave right now and come back in one hour. And if that list isn't back up on the microwave just exactly the way it was, I'm going to beat you within an inch of your life and throw you right out of here. Do you understand *that*–clearly?

"Now, that's one choice," Norman continued in a calmer tone of voice. "The other choice is for you to put the list back, and we'll become friends. That's the way I'd prefer it to be. You're good at what you do, and we should be teammates. It's up to you, Ed."

When Norman returned an hour later, the sign was back up on the wall. Afterward, he and Ed Bolling became good friends. "We overcame the hostility," Norman recalled. "Once he knew that I was for him and respected him, we were able to build a good relationship."

For the next year, Norm threw himself into his work, putting in long hours to master the details of every part of the operations of Jack-In-The-Box. What's the temperature of the fryers? How long should you leave the french fries in? What's the best way to interact with our suppliers? Essentially, Norman was learning the ropes of the restaurant business.

Peterson admired the energy with which Brinker approached his new job. So much so, in fact, that one day he casually asked Norman if he had any money. "Yeah," he responded. "How much do you want? Here's five dollars."

"No, no, no," said Peterson. "I meant to buy an interest in Jack-In-The-Box. One of the original four people who owned 20 percent has dropped out."

"How much is it," asked Norm.

"It's $3,500 for 20 percent. What do you say?"

It turned out that Norman and Maureen had exactly $3,500 in their savings account. When he told his wife what Peterson was offering, she said: "Go for it, if that's what you want to do." So, despite the fact that he had a new mouth to feed, Norm Brinker risked everything he had to become a general partner in Jack-In-The-Box.

At once, he began to concentrate on growing the business. He added tacos to the menu, and sales went up. He did some advertising, and sales went up. Then Norman went to Peterson with an expansion idea. "Say, how do you build more of these?" he inquired.

"You get landowners to build them and then lease them to you," said Bob.

"Hmmm. You mean if a person has a piece of property for sale," he asked, "instead of buying the property, you ask them to construct a building for you—and then you lease it from them?"

"Yes, that's right," responded Peterson.

"Wow," thought Norman. "We can do that until the cows come home."

So, putting his thoughts and skills into action, he began to expand away. Marvin Braddock recalled Norman's ability to negotiate: "He was a real horse trader," recalled Marvin. "I remember sitting in the backseat of his Chevy Impala while he and one real estate guy negotiated over a Jack-In-The-Box property. Norman got exactly what he wanted in short order. But he approached the fellow in a fair and honest manner. I think he had a fixed price in the back of his mind. If he got that or better, he'd be fine. But he wouldn't give in. He was willing to risk it all or lose it all based on that figure. He just wouldn't pay more than the property was worth. I had the feeling Norman enjoyed a good horse trade as much or more than securing property at a good price."

In less than two years, San Diego had fifteen Jack-In-The-Boxes, each one making a solid profit. And, by January of 1960, Norman had moved his family to Phoenix to expand the business further. Six months later, Norm had eight profitable Jack-In-The-Box restaurants there. And three years later, there were twenty-five units of Jack-In-The-Box in the Phoenix metropolitan area. Norman had learned the operations business to a T and polished the expansion process.

Interestingly, as things began to run smoothly in Arizona, Norman became a bit bored and found himself with some extra time on his hands. One afternoon he noticed a polo trophy on a friend's desk, and, a few days later, he was out on a polo field with a rented horse and a mallet. The next week, he purchased two horses and a small trailer. Norman had been working so hard the last few years, he'd almost forgotten the pure joy he received in being with horses. In addition, the competition involved in polo helped him expend some of the energy that he built up inside from the business.

And so it began. For the next three decades, the sport of polo would be a consistent part of Norm Brinker's life—helping him through times of personal difficulty, providing him a vehicle to meet new friends, traveling with him to new cities, and, as it turned out, transcending new jobs.

~

IN 1962, NORMAN'S FATHER, Gene, died at the age of eighty-three. Two years before, he had suffered a massive stroke and lived semi-disabled. Prior to that, Gene Brinker had never been sick a day in his life. He had always been in excellent physical condition—no aches, no pains, no flu, no colds, nothing. Norman had never even seen him sniffle.

"My father had a great influence on the way I lived my life," Norman recalled. "He not only taught me a lot about how to take care of myself, he also cared about me very much and always looked after me. I remember when I was sixteen years old, I'd sometimes sneak away to break broncos. When Dad saw me putting a saddle in the car without taking a horse, he knew where I was heading. Often, he'd follow me at a distance. And later I'd spot him in the crowd around the corral, but he'd never come around so as not to embarrass me in front of my friends. He'd stay in the background to make sure I was okay. He was just a great person."

Gene's death affected his son greatly. In addition to enjoying a very close bond with him, Norman had always considered his father invincible. Now, a jolt of the harsh reality of how quickly life could end would have a major impact on his future approach to life.

For nearly a year, Norm thought about what he wanted to do with his life. Eventually, he asked himself the following question: "When I am eighty-three, would I be sorrier if I went on my own and fizzled–or would I be sorrier if I stayed at Jack-In-The-Box and had not given myself a chance to see if I could or couldn't make it on my own?" The answer turned out to be an easy one. Norman knew that he would forever wonder if he could have been successful on his own.

In November 1963, Norman was asked to move to Houston to lead Jack-In-The-Box's expansion into Texas. Upon arriving, he decided to take all he had learned–operations, leasing, hiring, training, and developing–and see if he could be successful in a new territory. He called the following year his "master's course" in the restaurant business. And earn his degree he did. During that time, Norm opened ten restaurants in Houston and moved aggressively into the Dallas market with five more.

While successfully expanding Jack-In-The-Box, he saw many restaurants, such as Burger Chef, begin to fizzle. Consequently, he grew more and more confident that he could compete favorably with other chains–whether he was with a large company or on his own. He now knew that he'd be okay as part of a larger corporation even if he couldn't make it as an entrepreneur.

So, in early 1964, at the age of thirty-four, now with two young daughters (Cindy and Brenda) to support, Norman Brinker decided to go out on his own. He saw what he believed would be a terrific location and a great opportunity in Dallas for a restaurant similar to Oscar's. He'd call it Brink's Coffee Shop.

After thinking his plans through, Norm made the difficult call to Bob Peterson to tell him what he wanted to do. Peterson found it hard to believe, and talked about plans for going public and what that would mean to Norman. "I'm real disappointed to see you leave," he finally said. "But if that's what you really want to do, I'll help you any way I can. What do you need?"

"Well," he replied, "I'd like to come back to California and work in an Oscar's for a few months to refresh myself about the operations. What do you think?"

"Come on out," replied Peterson.

Before leaving, Norman formed a partnership with four other men to get his new restaurant under way. Then he approached the owner of the property about paying for the construction of the building and leasing it to the partnership. Everything moved like clockwork—just as it had at Jack-In-The-Box. When the foundation for the new restaurant was laid, Norm took off for San Diego.

Back at Oscar's, he learned how it was managed, how time cards were used, how people were paid. And he refreshed his memory on all the operations involved in running such a coffee shop.

Norman also asked Bob Peterson to buy out his 20 percent interest in Jack-In-The-Box. He was reminded again that Jack-In-The-Box would probably go public in a few years and that 20 percent would be worth a substantial sum of money when that happened. Still, Norman felt he had to take the risk and make the move now. So, he received a note from Peterson for eighty thousand dollars payable at the rate of six hundred dollars per month for about ten years. Norman reasoned that he could live on that money while he tried to make his restaurant successful. Besides, it was not a bad return on his original $3,500 investment of six years ago.

During the summer of 1964, Brink's made its debut at the corner of Gaston and Carroll avenues in east Dallas. And Norm did a bit of everything. He waited on tables; he was the cashier, the cook, the manager—and, once in a while, he even slept overnight in the coffee shop.

But being in the breakfast market was not as profitable as Norman had hoped. It was a lot of work for very little return—and it was difficult to maintain a reliable staff. Frequently, he'd receive a call at 5:30 or 6:00 in the morning informing him that one of his employees hadn't shown up for work and that the individual's telephone number was out of service. "It was hard," Norman would later recall, "to get someone else to come in and work at five-thirty in the morning when they weren't scheduled. So, on those days, I was the breakfast cook, busboy, and waiter."

~

IT DIDN'T TAKE NORMAN LONG to realize that his coffee shop would not make the grade. Business wasn't what it should have been. Customers did not flock to his new eatery in droves. And he was just squeaking by.

As reality began to set in, 1965 became a difficult year for Norm Brinker. His father was gone. He had given up perhaps $750,000 to $1 million guaranteed when Jack-In-The-Box went public. And for what? A modestly successful restaurant.

"It was one of the few times in my life," Norman would later recall, "when I didn't seem to have a clear sense of direction. I was searching for something to do. Should I stay in the restaurant business or possibly go into real estate?"

Norman found himself bored, discouraged, unexcited. He drifted into a period of inactivity where he had trouble responding to the outside influences of people he knew—as well as his own internal needs.

Norman Brinker needed something. But what was it?

BRINKER PRINCIPLES

- Base future sales success on references from satisfied customers. Exceed customer expectations.
- The first step in persuasion involves listening to others.
- Always be 100 percent straight and open with the people you seek to lead.
- Obtain a psychological commitment from others so they might be motivated from their own self-interest.
- Visit people in person and include them on your team.
- Be fair to people and involve them in the planning process.
- Once people know that you respect them and are for them, you will be able to build a lasting relationship.
- Put yourself in the shoes of the customer.
- Master the operations of your business—down to the smallest detail. Don't be afraid to start in the basement.
- Concentrate on growing the business.
- Evaluate all your options before making a life-changing decision.
- Don't be afraid to risk everything.

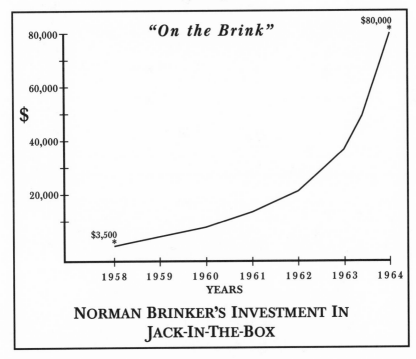

NORMAN BRINKER'S INVESTMENT IN JACK-IN-THE-BOX

5.

"*Mr. Brinker's condition is very grave. He might regain consciousness, but it could be days or weeks. I'm cautiously optimistic.*"

DR. PHIL WILLIAMS,
to the media, February 1993

"*I talked to him about everything that was going on every day. I played classical music for him. I turned on CNN every hour so he could hear the latest news. I treated him as if he were awake. I just wouldn't let myself believe that he was in as bad a shape as they said he was. I tried to will him into waking up.*"

NANCY BRINKER,
on her routine when Norman was in the coma

The Coma

....

The morning after the family's medical conference, Eric Brinker walked into the intensive care unit and was shocked to find his father packed in bags of ice from head to toe. "It was like he was in a refrigerator," said Eric. "They had towels over his head and ice literally everywhere. He looked like something from *Aliens*."

A few hours earlier, Norman's temperature had suddenly shot up to 106 degrees. The physician on duty explained to Nancy that the increase was extremely dangerous. "It's the body saying 'We're leaving.' We have to get the fever down as fast as possible."

By early evening, the doctors had won the battle as Norman's temperature began to approach normal. But then they noticed that, due to excess fluid built up in his lungs, Norm had developed a bad case of pneumonia. In addition to various medications, part of the treatment involved periodically vacuuming out Norman's lungs. It was a terrible process that Eric would watch just to be certain he knew what they were doing to his dad. "As they performed the process, he would be hanging over the bed on his stomach," recalled Eric. "The vacuum made inhuman sounds and caused him to vomit. It was more like a reflex action because he didn't have anything in his stomach."

Doctors also noticed that their patient's left eye had become red and swollen. The dirt that had impaired his vision during the polo match had now caused a serious infection, threatening his sight. Antibiotics and eyedrops were prescribed to clear up the problem. In addition, the ICP monitor in Norman's forehead sounded intermittently–alerting the doctors to swelling. When the pressure increased too much, a diuretic drug would be administered to counter the negative effect.

After about a week, Norm's condition stabilized. But while in intensive care, he was never breathing on his own–a mechanical respirator kept him alive. Nevertheless, the stabilization of Norman's condition heartened Nancy. "Every day that went by gave us hope," she would comment later.

In the early going, however, every day that went by caused the investment community some serious anxiety. After all, the chairman and chief executive officer (CEO) of a major global corporation had been seriously hurt.

On Saturday, two days after the accident, the president of Brinker International, Ron McDougall, and Norman's personal attorney, Don Godwin, traveled to Florida to confer with Nancy and prepare a press release. At first, they had no idea whether Norman, who was still undergoing intense testing and examination, was going to recover. So the decision was made that as long as he was stable, they would assume that he was going to be okay.

By midafternoon on Friday, the three had prepared the following press statement, which was released after the stock markets closed:

Norman E. Brinker, chairman and chief executive officer of Brinker International, Inc., was involved in a polo accident at the Palm Beach Polo Club in Florida on Thursday, Jan. 21, 1993. Exact details of the incident are not yet known.

Brinker is in the hospital, where he is being treated for his injuries.

His vital signs are stable, and the prognosis appears to be favorable.

During the last hour of trading on the New York Stock Exchange, word seemed to have slipped out that something was up, as Brinker shares fell seventy-five cents. Other than that, however, the company's stock price was not substantially affected.

On Sunday, just two days later, the Brinker International board met in Dallas and named McDougall interim chairman and CEO until the full extent of Norman's injuries became clear. In one of his first interviews, McDougall was asked what he was going to change—to which he answered: "Nothing. We'll just execute our plan. And we'll make the calls we would have made if Norman were here." He then asked all employees of Brinker to deliver the best quarter in the company's history. "Let's do it for Norman," he told them.

Just as Brinker executives did not overreact to Norman's injury, neither did most financial analysts. *The Wall Street Journal,* for example, reported that "Mr. Brinker's strength wasn't just entrepreneurial, but in building the team, in creating the corporate culture. [And there should be little] immediate impact on investors, because the company's growth plans and strategies were arrived at not just by Mr. Brinker, but by his management team."

Still, there was tremendous interest in Norman's condition as the public and press clamored for information. People called from all over the country. "We received many calls from restaurant managers," remembered Ellie and Marvin Goodman. "Olive Garden, Chili's, Outback Steakhouse, Steak & Ale, Burger King, Godfather's Pizza, TGI Friday's—you name it, and we heard from them."

At a downstairs waiting area near the intensive care unit at St. Mary's, the family organized chairs around three pay phones—which would ring all the time. "Just as soon as you'd hang up one phone," recalled Eric Brinker, "it would ring again." As they answered the calls, each held a copy of the official press release so that they would remain consistent in what they told the press. Within two or three days of the official announcement's release, the onslaught of calls began to taper off. For some reason, though, Norman's accident captured the media's fancy. The story was recounted all over the world–and certain renegade members of the press began to cause problems.

Some reporters made up excuses to gain access to the ICU. Others tried to sneak in. One man even dressed up as a minister and claimed he wanted to pray for Mr. Brinker.

In another instance, Eric was down near the hospital's main entrance mailing some thank-you notes for his mother (who was responding to some of the hundreds of letters, faxes, and flowers that had poured in) when he noticed a man speaking to the receptionist: "Hey, where's Norm Brinker?" he asked. When she steadfastly refused to give him any information, he responded: "It's okay, I'm an old friend of his."

Later, this same fellow dressed up like a doctor and walked into the ICU carrying a camera. Eric recognized him and immediately informed his grandmother. Ellie Goodman then jumped in front of the reporter and started poking her right index finger into his chest between the tubes of a stethoscope. "You get the hell out of here right now, or we're going to call the cops! In fact, don't move. We're going to have you thrown out right now!" With that, the impersonator ran out of the room, never to be seen again.

After that incident, Nancy had Norman moved to a corner room in the intensive care unit that offered more difficult access. She also requested that a hospital security guard be stationed at the door to make certain that no unauthorized personnel slipped by.

Hospital administrators provided Nancy Brinker with an upstairs suite because she would not leave her husband's side. But half the time, she loaned it out to other patients' families who had to sleep all night in the waiting room because their loved ones were in dire condition.

Every night she spoke with Dr. Williams in Dallas to give him daily progress and status reports. He told her that he was encouraged by the fact that Norman had passed without difficulties the seventy-two-hour and ninety-six-hour points after the accident, when swelling or increased intercranial pressure can reach its maximum. From these conversations, Dr. Williams was able to help keep the mass media at bay. "Mr. Brinker's condition is very grave," he said to the press. "He might regain consciousness, but it could be days or weeks. I'm cautiously optimistic."

Nancy also sought advice from several trusted people. She called her good friend Sandy Alexander, who had suffered a very serious head injury and recovered after a period of time in a coma. "Don't stop talking to him," said Mrs. Alexander. "Don't stop touching him. Trust me, it makes a difference."

Dr. Williams had made the same suggestion with some added insight: "When you talk to him," he said, "notice the EKG and the blood pressure monitor and see if there's any change. If there is, that will be a sign that the coma is starting to lighten up a bit."

When Norman's condition stabilized, a prompt and efficient routine developed. Every morning, doctors examined him. They moved his limbs, checked his pupils, and asked him to respond to their voice commands. Then, at Nancy's request, the medical staff dressed Norman fully.

Each day from 11 A.M. to 2 P.M., he would be taken out for a CAT scan or a Magnetic Resonance Imaging (MRI). As seven or eight assistants wheeled the gurney down the corridor, one person would perform Norman's respiration all the way to the lab by manually squeezing a balloon.

A physical therapist came down to intensive care every few hours to massage and work Norman's arms and legs so they would not atrophy. In between those visits, people sitting with Norman did the same thing. "Other than when he was having his CAT scans," Nancy recalled, "he didn't go for twenty or thirty minutes without someone moving his arms and legs."

Actually, Nancy Brinker made certain that there was someone with Norman all the time–whether it was family, friends, or medical personnel. For example, George Olivas would arrive at midday after he had finished playing polo. "Nancy asked me to talk to him, keep his blood circulating, give him massages, touch him a lot," said George, "which I was only too happy to do." Olivas talked about polo matches he had just played–who won and how it went. He spoke about things they would usually discuss if Norm were awake. "I told him the status of the horses and how they were doing," recalled George. "I'd mention all their names: Juanita, Kachobie, Roberta, Little Delta, Ashley, and the others."

Frequently, Norman's daughter, Brenda, sat in the room alone and held her father's hand. Every now and then, almost at regular intervals, she'd feel Norman's hand twitch, or jerk, or jump. Sometimes it would happen to his entire body–other times, his hands would start twitching uncontrollably and stop a few minutes later. "And then," remembered Brenda, "only the muscles around his eyes and his eyelids would twitch. I just wanted to shake him and yell: 'Wake up, Dad!'"

Ten days after the accident, the family noticed that Norman was getting very thin. Nancy mentioned it to the doctors and recommended they increase his nutritional supplement. At first, they were skeptical. But Nancy told them that Norm had always burned calories at amazing rates–and that she felt he'd starve to death if something wasn't done. The physicians conferred and then increased the supplement.

While many friends and members of the family came in to sit with Norman, it was Nancy who monitored everything that happened to her husband. Her temporary home was his room in the ICU. There she had placed symbols of many different religions: St. Anthony, St. Jude, the Jewish mezuzah, a Hindu prayer object, and others. Nancy was with him almost every moment from the time of the accident. "I talked to him about everything that was going on every day," she said. "I played classical music for him. I turned on CNN every hour so he could hear the latest news. I treated him as if he were awake. I just wouldn't let myself believe that he was in as bad shape as they said he was. I tried to will him into waking up."

Nancy played Sousa marches and other patriotic songs in the morning. In the afternoon, it was Handel–and at night Chopin. "These were the things that his mother had shared with him when he was little," said Nancy. "I hoped he would respond to them and recover more quickly."

Moreover, Nancy felt it was important for Norman to hear the voices of friends and colleagues who were not able to make it to Florida. So, she tape-recorded messages from people in the company who wanted to wish Norman well.

One friend who did make it to see Norman while he was in the coma was Ross Perot, who flew down for a visit with Dr. Williams. "His eyes were closed, and he was not responsive. But every now and then he'd squeeze my hand," recalled Perot. "I talked to him about things he liked to do–particularly those that involved speed–like horses and motorcycles. I'd also tell him stories and try to give him reasons for getting well."

In addition, Perot told Norm that if he didn't hurry up and get back to work, Ross would have to fill in for him at the office. Before leaving Dallas, he had gone into a Chili's restaurant and found his table swarmed with emotional employees who wanted to get an update on Norman. "When I said I was going down to visit him in the hospital," he recalled, "they asked me to come outside and pose for a picture–and then they asked me to deliver it personally."

Perot had the picture (in which he was surrounded by a number of female employees) enlarged to poster size and held it up in the hospital room. "It's tough work, Brink," a grinning Ross told Norman, "but somebody's got to do it."

Before Perot left the hospital, he met privately with Nancy. "You know, Nancy," he said, "I've had the privilege of knowing many of the great people of our time. Norm is one of the most honest, ethical people I've ever known. I trust him completely, and so does everyone who has worked with him. He is also one of the most effective leaders and motivators I have ever worked with. The people in his companies not only admire, trust, and respect him—they love him. I don't know anyone who is more kind, caring, or generous in helping people in need.

"Norm is very special," continued Ross. "And you are very special, too, Nancy. You saved Norm's life. You've been here night and day at his side. You've been a source of strength and comfort to everyone who loves him—at a time when all of us would have fully understood if you were too grief-stricken to function."

At this point, Nancy started to get a little choked up, and Ross noticed tears in her eyes for the first time. Then, with a wry sense of humor that perhaps only a Texan could understand, Ross said: "Nancy, there is absolutely no chance we are going to lose Norm. He is going to make a full recovery—there's no doubt about it."

Nancy looked at him intensely: "Why do you say that," she asked.

"Because only the good die young," quipped Perot, "and you and I both know that Brinker is BAD! Brinker's going to live forever!"

Nancy broke out in the convivial laugh for which she's known: "You're absolutely right," she said, "Norman is BAD, and you and I both *know* it. But let's keep it a secret between us."

Perot laughed and replied, "Remember, Nancy, Noah was six hundred years old when he built the ark for the flood. Norm is just a boy. He'll get through this, thanks to you."

On the plane ride back to Dallas, Ross had a word with Dr. Williams. "Phil," he said, "Norm has always been in excellent physical condition. Doesn't that enhance his chances for recovery?"

"That's one of the principal reasons he will recover," said the doctor matter-of-factly.

"Any reservations?" asked Perot.

"Ross," responded Williams, "there's one thing you've got to remember. A person who is sixty-two does not heal as quickly as a person who is nineteen."

"Why not?" said Perot seriously.

"Your cells are older." Phil grinned as both men broke into laughter.

"Trust me, Ross," said Dr. Williams finally. "Brinker will be back."

∽

ON SUNDAY MORNING in Palm Beach, thousands of people lined up to participate in a 5K run to benefit breast cancer research. It was the Susan G. Komen Foundation's "Race for the Cure"–founded by Nancy Brinker in 1982 and named for her sister. Before the starting gun sounded, a voice on the public address system informed everyone that Nancy was unable to participate in the event because she was at the hospital with her husband. And for the next sixty seconds, the crowd stood absolutely silent as they prayed for Norman's recovery. "You could have heard a pin drop among five thousand people," a friend told Nancy.

Later that afternoon, the finals of the Challenge Cup were held at the Palm Beach Polo and Country Club. The Rev. John Mangrum also led a prayer over the public address system as 4,500 fans stood and bowed their heads. "Watch over your son and servant, Norman, oh Lord," he said. "And bring him back to us in life."

6

"I'm not afraid to fail. I'm not afraid to
make mistakes. For me, if you take away
the risk, life would go kind of flat."

NORMAN BRINKER,
on why he risked everything to start Steak & Ale

"From the very beginning, I wanted this to
become a substantial group of restaurants.
I wanted Steak & Ale to be something
different—more the atmosphere I'd like for
my personal friends...I'm in the people
business, you know—not just the food
business."

NORMAN BRINKER,
on his original vision for Steak & Ale

Steak & Ale and Bennigan's

It wasn't long at all before the spark returned, and Norman was looking ahead to what the future held. Brink's Coffee Shop was not making a good profit, and Norm realized that if he were to stay in the restaurant business, he would need something with shorter hours and a higher ticket average. It was time to move on to something new, he believed. It was time to make something happen.

An old friend from Arizona persuaded Norman to try his hand at real estate. "I went back to Phoenix for eight months," he said. "I played polo and made tons of money. But the real estate business just didn't excite me. So I began to think about restaurants again."

As always, Norman's natural ability and endless energy took over. In Phoenix one evening, he went out to eat dinner at a new local restaurant called Cork & Cleaver. It had the type of operation and service style he had been contemplating. First of all, its atmosphere and operations seemed to fall somewhere in between a fast-food joint and an elegant restaurant—it was friendly, fun, and not over-priced. There was also a salad bar area where customers fixed their own salads and took them back to their tables. The restaurant's menu was printed on a real meat cleaver—which was something totally different. And most important, the place was packed—with a long line of people angling out the door into the parking lot.

Norman was really intrigued by the operation. He had become friends with Cork & Cleaver's owners, Peter Green and Tom Fleck, while playing polo and decided to approach them about a franchise opportunity. While they weren't interested in that proposition, they generously invited Norman back to learn their operations if he truly wanted to open a similar restaurant someplace else.

Well, he certainly did. And after returning to Dallas, there was no doubt in his mind about the Cork & Cleaver concept. After listening, learning, and talking with people he trusted, a new and broad vision began to formulate.

"Prior to the sixties, people were looking at restaurants as places to eat, a place to get food—and that was it," said Norman. "But I saw this niche between fast food and fine dining. Cork & Cleaver had tapped into it on a local basis and was thriving. But there were no restaurants on a national scale where you could get outstanding full-menu table service at prices only a few dollars more than Jack-In-The-Box or McDonald's."

Norman's new vision was that of a restaurant atmosphere with more merriment; one that would be fun to visit *and* offer good food; one where everybody dressed in casual clothes. "It should have very reasonable prices," he thought, "with waiters who met the guests on an even keel and talked to them as friends." Essentially, it was the idea of casual dining at a very reasonable price.

Norman decided to build a steak restaurant, Mediterranean in theme with a name something like El Toro or El Bravo. And, just as he had learned at Jack-In-The-Box and Brink's, he went out and found a good location and then approached the landowner, Mr. Stanley Klein, about building his new-style restaurant. After a few hours of enthusiastic persuasion, Klein decided to go for it.

Norman then went to a friend and partner for financial support. Both put up $5,500 and co-signed for an equipment loan of sixty thousand dollars from a large Dallas bank. Their initial debt-to-equity ratio was 98 to 2, and all of Norm's money was sunk into the enterprise. Such a risk made him slightly nervous, but he plowed ahead anyway. "I'm not afraid to fail," he told his partner. "I'm not afraid to make mistakes. For me, if you take away the risk, life would go kind of flat. We'll make this one work."

Plans progressed rapidly, and, as a Monday meeting to begin construction of the building approached, Norman flew to San Diego for the weekend and called on his old friend and mentor Bob Peterson. Norman explained to Bob in some detail what his plans were. "What are you going to name the restaurant?" asked Peterson after hearing about the concept.

"Well," he said, "we haven't come up with a name yet."

"Why don't you call it Steak & Ale?" said Peterson.

"Bob," responded Norm, "I can't call it Steak & Ale. That's not Mediterranean-sounding."

And just like Gene Brinker had said about his son's rabbit enterprise some twenty years earlier, Peterson retorted: "Norman, that's your problem."

So, all the way back on the plane from San Diego to Dallas, Norm kept thinking "Steak & Ale, Steak & Ale." "Boy, that makes sense," he thought. "It creates an image, a visual image. It is truly unique. I like it." Upon his return, he and Maureen went out to a local theater to view the new movie, *Tom Jones*. After seeing the feast scene, Norm decided to give his restaurant an old English theme—with "gusto" eating, corn-on-the-cob, big baked potatoes, and big juicy steaks. So, while he stayed with his original decision to build a steak restaurant, Norman's tendency toward flexibility led to the old English theme with a new name. Now he hoped his colleagues would be equally receptive.

On Monday morning, for the planned signing of the construction contract, Norman met with the building contractor, the architect, Klein, and the two men he had hired to run the restaurant, Harold Deem and Dan Landers, who brought with them a bottle of champagne to celebrate the contract signing. "I've got a little problem, fellas," he began. "The restaurant is not going to be Mediterranean. It's going to be English—and it's going to be called Steak & Ale. Sorry about this."

Stanley Klein's reaction was quick and accommodating: "Norman," he said, "if you think it would be better, that's fine with me. I'm very nervous about a restaurant company, anyway." Deem and Landers both said that if they had waited this long, they could wait a bit longer. The builder replied: "Gosh, Norman, I already bid this once, I guess I'll just have to re-bid it. That'll take a couple of weeks—but it shouldn't make any difference in the price." That left only the architect, who said: "It'll take me three to four weeks to redraw this, and it'll cost $1,500 to do it."

Norman's response was quick and to the point: "I don't have $1,500," he said. "I've committed every dollar I have to buy equipment and such. Tell you what I'll do, I'll pay you one hundred dollars a month for ten months. At the end of the tenth month, if I'm making money, I'll pay you one thousand more. If I'm not making money, and you'll know if I'm not, we'll call it even."

"Well," said Charles Little, the architect, "that sounds like a fair deal to me. Let's do that and move forward."

Then they all loaded into a car and drove out to the old Dumphey Hotel in Dallas, which had an old English design. "There's no need to be making a lot of new designs," Norman said to Little. "Make it just like this—*just like this.*"

As construction of the first Steak & Ale began during the summer of 1965, Norman set about attending to the details of his new enterprise. From the very beginning, his vision was to build a substantial group of restaurants. As such, he was careful not to end up micromanaging the first restaurant, because he wanted it to operate on its own as he opened others. That's the principal reason Norman offered the top management job to Harold Deem, whom he had hired several years before as a supervisor at Jack-In-The-Box.

For several months, Norman and Harold kicked around ideas involving operations and atmosphere for the restaurant. Good food was a must. There would be a limited menu of steaks, vegetables (especially corn-on-the-cob), and hot bread. Norman was also particularly excited by the idea of a salad bar. It was kind of fun to get up and create your own salad. And it added to the ambience of informality and friendliness that Norman hoped to create. "Essentially, I wanted my customers to feel that we were happy they were there," recalled Norm. "Guests don't feel welcome when people are just standing around with a wooden smile."

He also knew that the customers wouldn't be impatient for service if they were free to build their own salads as they pleased. That also meant fewer trips for the waiters. All told, it would allow them to move more people in and out each evening—which translated into a better dining experience and, subsequently, a better bottom line.

Harold Deem went out to Phoenix for a couple of months to learn the system in detail from the folks at Cork & Cleaver, who, as they had previously said, were very willing to share their knowledge. While Deem was mastering details of the operations, Norman felt very positive about employing young, enthusiastic waiters and waitresses and dressing them in nineteenth century English time-period costumes. The only question he had to answer now was: "Where do I get young people who also happen to be intelligent and reliable?"

After mulling it over for a day or two, Norm thought of employing college students—which was essentially unheard of in the restaurant industry at the time. So he called the job placement office at Southern Methodist University in north Dallas and explained that he had openings for twelve or fifteen people to work part-time in the evenings. "They were very excited to help me until I told them the name of the restaurant was Steak & Ale," he recalled.

"Steak & Ale!" they repeated. "Do you serve liquor?"

"Yes I do," said Norman.

"Oh, well," came the reply, "then we can't help you."

At first Norm thought he was out of luck. But then he remembered his days as a door-to-door salesman when he could persuade people very well once he was face-to-face with them. So he decided to go down to the SMU campus personally and see whether he could make any headway. But rather than going to the administration's office, Norman went out to a fraternity house.

"I just got out of my car, went up and knocked on the door," he recalled. "When someone answered, I went into my pitch, which was something like this: 'Say, I'm opening a restaurant that's going to be called Steak & Ale. All the waiters, waitresses, and hostesses will be dressed up like it was in mid-1800s England—just like in the movie *Tom Jones*—with knee pants and a white billowing shirt. I've got openings for ten or fifteen people—both male and female. The jobs don't pay a salary, you'll work for tips. But the hours are only at night, and they're flexible—so you could go to class during the days. Do you think anybody here would be interested in a job like that?'"

"Well, the reaction was more than enthusiastic," remembered Norman. "The next day, forty or fifty students showed up for interviews. I picked eight or ten men and five or six women. It was wonderful—and it was no different than when I used to sell cutlery. I simply sat down and talked to the people personally, and it had positive results once again."

Prior to Steak & Ale, most eating establishments did not employ college students as waiters and waitresses. But it was a new trend that would soon be emulated all across the country. And it was a good deal for everybody involved. The restaurants received the talents of the students—and the students were able to work flexible hours in a meaningful job that paid well enough to help them through college.

So, when customers were seated at a Steak & Ale restaurant, they were greeted by an upbeat young person who handed each customer a meat cleaver with a menu on it and said: "Hi! I'm Terry, and I'll be your waiter tonight."

The Steak & Ale restaurant was an instant hit—thriving and prosperous from the first night of business. And Norman quickly opened a second, a third—and then set out to expand nationwide. At the time, nothing could compete with his new restaurant chain—because there just wasn't anything like it out there. Norm Brinker had truly created an innovative concept that filled a tremendous void in the dining market.

Norman's new niche, later to be dubbed "casual dining," immediately began taking away customers from all other levels of the restaurant business: fast-food places, coffee shops, and fine-dining restaurants. And naturally, the idea was seized upon by the industry at large. All of a sudden, similar restaurants started popping up all across the country, including Red Lobster and TGI Friday's. But as many were to find out, there was more to success in this new niche than met the eye.

Everybody went to Steak & Ale to learn how it was done. As a matter of fact, Norman's new restaurant chain became something of a "casual dining" university with Norman as the dean. And, just like the owners of Cork & Cleaver—and Bob Peterson before them—Norm answered all questions openly and tried to help every person who wanted to learn.

In so doing, he created significant opportunities for future entrepreneurs who, through Steak & Ale, learned the operations and management style of Norman Brinker's creative breakthrough. In a very real sense, Steak & Ale was to the restaurant industry what Ford's Model T was to the automobile industry—it was revolutionary.

~

TO NEARLY EVERYONE WHO ASKED the secret of his success, Norman stressed two major strategies. "First, you've got to get the best people possible to work with you," he advocated. "People who are bright, energetic, honest, persistent, and flexible." And hire bright people he did. For example, some of the individuals Norman attracted to Steak & Ale later went on to run major chains in their own right. There were Chris Sullivan and Bob Basham of Outback Steakhouses, Wally Doolin of TGI Fridays, George Biel of Houston's Restaurants, Richard Rivera of Longhorn Steaks, Fred Hipp of Houlihan's, Mike Jenkins of VICORP, Dick Frank of Showbiz Pizza, and Lou Neeb of Casa Olé—to name a few. "Hiring such great people," said Norman, "allows you to exceed customer expectations—which should always be a constant goal."

Norm also emphasized the importance of creating and maintaining an internal culture that was "can-do," enthusiastic, and enjoyable. "Having bright, young people around takes care of that right off the bat," he would say. "But it's also important to establish a clear culture quickly so you know who you are, what you are, and where you are going."

Furthermore, Brinker insisted on the highest degree of honesty and integrity in every way. "For instance," he would explain, "if a supplier ever ships us an additional case of something, we quickly call and tell them. And then, when we subsequently call and say we've been shorted, they unequivocally know it's true."

Norman's dedication to high ethical standards really paid off in the early 1970s when he turned down a number of alcohol purveyors who offered free barrels of beer or extra fifths of liquor if Steak & Ale's restaurants would purchase a certain brand. At the time, his company was doing such a good business that Norman calculated it could mean an extra $300,000 a year or more in profits. He said he would do it as long as they would leave a credit invoice each time a keg or a bottle was given. "Oh, no," came the response, "we'll just slide it under the table to you. It's okay. Everybody's doing it." Even though he knew the competition was participating, Norm turned it down.

Six months later, an agent from the Bureau of Alcohol, Tobacco and Firearms came by to see him. "Mr. Brinker," he said, "we're investigating companies who serve alcoholic beverages and have been taking kickbacks from the distilleries and beer companies." Norman welcomed the investigation with open arms, because he knew he had nothing to hide. However, one of his competitors was in the midst of going public, and a similar investigation squelched the entire deal. "Whenever I'm asked to comment on the culture of our corporation," said Norman, "I always tell that story and conclude by saying that the foundation of your company's culture must always be high, ethical behavior."

Another important aspect of Steak & Ale's culture was the casualness of dress and conversation. "We wanted everyone to know that they worked in a people-oriented company," recalled Norman, "where they were free to be direct, free to be themselves, free to enjoy their jobs. I believe that makes all the difference in the world."

Part of that freedom also involved a concerted effort to push authority and responsibility as far down in the organization as possible. "You need to give people the freedom to try out their own ideas," Norman would advise, "even if it means that they fail a time or two."

"But, even more important," he'd continue, "you have to make people feel as though they are true partners in your enterprise. And the only way to do that is to share the wealth."

To Norm Brinker, sharing the wealth meant exactly that. His partner at Steak & Ale had a full 50 percent interest— and key people were given 2 to 5 percent of the company right away. Early on, though, Norman was careful not to give too much interest away, because there would be too little left to dole out when the enterprise grew larger.

For the young waiters and waitresses, Steak & Ale created a tip-sharing pool. "The waiters would pay 10 percent of whatever tips they made into the pool, which would then be distributed to the busboys," Norm explained. "That created a true team effort. The busboys really stepped up service, which led to better tips and more money—not to mention terrific customer satisfaction."

Norman's process for restaurant ownership and management was also designed on a partnership basis. As the company began to expand, joint ventures were set up for each Steak & Ale restaurant, with the idea that the owners could sell back their interest to the home office when the company later went public. "We would set people up, help them with the financing, and train them in operations and management," Norman recalled. "They would furnish 100 percent of the capital—and we would retain 20 percent of the business. It was a win-win situation for everybody involved."

∼

ABOUT THE TIME Steak & Ale was rolling into a major expansion, Maureen began having some lower back pains. After extensive testing, she was found to have cancer and immediately underwent major surgery. The doctors believed they had gotten it all, but exactly one year later, she began experiencing abdominal pains. A subsequent checkup revealed that the cancer had spread to her stomach.

As he tried to balance both Maureen's personal situation with managing a growing chain of restaurants, Norman began to feel an increasing amount of stress. Friends noted that his emotions seemed ready to erupt in a violent explosion. Ironically, such an outburst occurred at Steak & Ale during the Christmas holidays in 1968 as he was hosting a party for employees of Brink's Coffee Shop, which was still in business.

While the celebration was being held upstairs, Norman went down to the main part of the restaurant to mingle with his customers. He entered one area just in time to see ice being thrown across the room by one of eight rugged-looking men who had obviously been drinking heavily. Norman went up to the culprit and said: "Hey, fella, that just won't work. Why don't you come on outside and get some fresh air?"

"Sure," said the man who was about six inches taller than Norm and outweighed him by about fifty pounds. "Let's go."

As the two walked toward the exit, the inebriated customer stopped in front of the bar's swinging western doors and informed Norman that he had changed his mind and was going back to his table. "No, no, you're not going to go back," said Norm. "You're going to have to leave." When he refused, Norman walked through the swinging doors and into the bar to call the police. The fellow followed and called Norm "a really filthy name."

"As I began to dial, I got about three numbers down and hung up the phone. 'What did you call me?' I asked him. And when he repeated it, I slugged him and he went flying back through those swinging doors and fell into the vestibule there."

At the sound of the crash, the rest of the man's pals came out—as did all the young waiters, busboys, and dishwashers. The silence of the standoff was finally broken when one of the waiters began asking loudly: "Who's going to pay the check, who's going to pay the check?" Fortunately, the leader of the group said he would pay the check and then leave.

After things died down, Norm walked outside with a bottle of champagne and gave it to the men and wished them well. "I'm certainly glad this didn't end up in a brawl—or none of us would have had any fun," he told them. "Merry Christmas, everybody."

As Norman walked back into the restaurant, he distinctly remembered being worried. "Boy," he told Harold Deem, "I hit that guy as hard as I could but didn't knock him out. I'm a long way from being powerhouse enough to start a fight like that. A few more of them, and we could have had a really major fiasco."

After that night, Norm resolved never to lose his temper again, anywhere—whether it was in a restaurant or on the polo field. And Harold Deem, who was there managing the restaurant, later recalled that it was very uncharacteristic for Norman to ever do anything like that. "I believe that the stress associated with his wife's illness played a heavy part in that punch he threw," Harold surmised.

Despite her difficult illness, Maureen continued an ambitious and active schedule. She was on the advisory staff of Wilson sporting goods, and she continued to travel as a television commentator for major professional events, including Davis Cup matches, Wimbledon, and the Australian Open. She would not, however, be away from her family more than ten days at any one time, nor more than six weeks each year, and never on major holidays.

While in Dallas, Maureen completed her history degree at Southern Methodist University. She had not received her degree in San Diego because of Norman's career and the birth of their daughters. And each year, when school was out, Maureen would coach young people on the finer points of tennis.

Norman essentially lost a year of major progress at Steak & Ale by taking Maureen to specialists around the world in an attempt to find a cure for her disease. His primary focus at the time was to save her–and, to that end, he did everything he could think of.

After the Christmas holidays in 1968, Norm took Maureen to the Memorial Sloan-Kettering Institute in New York for ten days of tests. On the last day there, doctors informed them of the final prognosis. "Maureen," said one physician, "what they're doing in Dallas is the same treatment we would provide. You should go home and enjoy yourself. We believe you've already had your best days."

They both knew exactly what that meant. But as soon as the doctor made that statement, Maureen looked at the clock on the wall and said: "Oh, it's three minutes to six. I've got to go up and visit my friend before they close visiting hours."

"Maureen had met an elderly woman who was terrified of undergoing a cataract operation. That's where she was going," said Norman. "Sometimes I can still see her walking down the hall–in her slippers and a pink bathrobe–to visit that lady."

When Maureen came home from the hospital for her last few weeks, Norman had a special hospital bed placed downstairs in the living room near a bright bay window with a pretty view. A trained nurse tended to her around the clock, but the cancer took its toll quickly. Her last days were filled with contentment and peace, surrounded by her family.

On June 19, 1969, on the eve of Wimbledon, Maureen Connolly Brinker passed away as she had lived: quietly, softly—and with grace. Thousands of letters and telegrams flooded the Brinker residence expressing condolences and stating how much of a positive influence Maureen had on people's lives the world over. The flag at Wimbledon was lowered to half-staff. She left behind her devastated husband and two daughters, Cindy and Brenda, ages nine and eleven. She was thirty-four years old.

∼

SHAKEN AND DEEPLY SADDENED, Norman was struggling for sustenance and direction. He never really believed Maureen would die until just before it happened. "And neither did she," he recalled. "We were married for thirteen years, and she was very involved in every aspect of my life. It was a hard time for me."

Just when things were at their lowest for Norman, support arrived from the one person he had always been able to count on. Kathryn Brinker moved from Roswell to Dallas to be near her son and granddaughters. While she wanted to help, Kathryn did not want to live with her son. "I'll get an apartment," she told him.

Her reasoning was twofold: She was a fiercely independent woman and wanted to be on her own; but she also did not want to disturb her granddaughters' arrangement with Maureen's mother, Jessemine Connolly, who had been living with the Brinkers for the past several months. Mrs. Connolly would eventually stay for two more years to help with the girls—an act of love for which Norman would be forever grateful.

After Kathryn settled into her new apartment, she disappeared for a few days. "I was worried about her," said Norman, "but I should have known better." When he finally reached her by telephone, he asked her to go to lunch with him. "No," she said, "I'm too busy."

When Norm asked her how that could happen so fast, she replied: "You know that fellow, Ross Perot? Well, he's done that wonderful thing to get food to our Vietnam veterans. He receives hundreds and hundreds of letters each day, and I've been in his office answering them on a voluntary basis."

"Well, that's my mother," thought Norman. "She's going to be able to take care of herself as usual."

In his own way, Norm also took care of himself after Maureen's death. Unable to just stand around and feel bad all the time, he threw himself into his work by concentrating fully on the rapid growth of Steak & Ale. Norman hired his old college friend (and colleague at Jack-In-The-Box), Marvin Braddock, to come work at Steak & Ale to manage the company's purchasing and distribution needs. Then he resolved to take his company public. "I really wanted to build more sites very quickly," Norman recalled, "but we needed more equity. At that point, we were still running a 98 to 2 debt-to-equity ratio—one that the bank often brought to my attention."

Even though the restaurant industry had a lousy market in 1969 and 1970, Norman took his idea of going public to his friend, Dan Cook, a principal at the Dallas offices of Goldman Sachs. While Cook was skeptical at first because of the debt and size of Steak & Ale, Norm's persistence and enthusiasm won him over. "Okay, okay, okay," said Cook finally. "Tell you what, if you can earn a million dollars after tax, we can take you public. We've never done it for a company as small as yours, but we will do it for you, Norman, assuming that an in-depth appraisal goes well." So, in 1971, Steak & Ale went public with twenty-eight restaurants and $1,012,000 in earnings.

Shortly thereafter, Norman started to expand nationally by placing Steak & Ale units in many states. As they grew, the company used the name "Jolly Ox" in states where it was against the law to use "Ale" or any other reference to liquor in the name of a restaurant. Those areas included California, Indiana, Virginia, and Canada, among others.

And wherever a Steak & Ale or a Jolly Ox restaurant opened, Norman was there on the first day. He believed it was important to get things off to a good start with personal human contact. Moreover, he was able to gauge the responses and opinions of his customers in various places around the country.

This had always seemed to be a consistent part of his business philosophy. "Norman would constantly walk around the restaurant talking to the customers," recalled Harold Deem, his operating partner, "asking them how the food was, how they liked the restaurant, if they were enjoying themselves, and where they would have gone had they not come to Steak & Ale."

One day he walked up to a table occupied by a middle-aged Texan and his wife. "Hello, I'm Norm Brinker," he said. "I hope you're enjoying everything this evening. Is the food good?"

"Hi, nice to see ya'," the man replied. "I'm Ross Perot. This is my wife, Margot. Food's great. Everything's fine! Terrific! Fine!"

"Oh," said Norman, "do you know my mother, Kathryn Brinker? She's a volunteer down at your office."

"Yeah, of course," said Perot. "She's a great lady and a hard worker. Nobody else in the place can keep up with her. So *you're* the son she's always talking about. Well, sit down for a few minutes." Perot and Brinker liked each other right off the bat. And their friendship would be lifelong.

Norman met many people in the same manner. And as his business expanded, so did the ways he obtained feedback from his customers. "I had this habit," he recalled, "of asking people as they came out, 'Hey, what kind of restaurant is this?'—as though I hadn't been there. And nearly everyone would stop and tell me exactly what they thought. It was good feedback—it was honest and candid."

By employing this practice on a regular and wide-ranging basis, Norm was able to keep track of trends in the marketplace. Doing so felt natural and seemed to fit with his general personality. He enjoyed being around people—and he constantly studied human nature. The restaurant business satisfied Norman's curiosity, his need to be with people, and his innate drive to create something of lasting value. Recall that when he decided to go to work for Bob Peterson at Jack-In-The-Box, he told Maureen that it sounded like fun. And fun is exactly what it turned out to be—most of the time.

One serious crisis occurred in 1974 during the Arab oil embargo, when people weren't going anywhere, least of all out to dinner, because they couldn't get gas. As a result, Steak & Ale's stock fell from a high of fifty dollars per share to a low of six dollars. But curiously, Norman didn't seem to panic at all.

"We never heard him talk about the value of the stock," said Carl Hays. "We never heard him say that he just lost, say, ten million dollars in stock. With Norman, it was: 'Okay, our sales are down. What do we do to get them up?' He talked about getting better, planning better, and executing better. And he never did lose his sense of humor. Actually, because of Norman's positive attitude, we never really doubted that we'd come out of the crisis in good shape."

In general, the restaurant business is very risky in the short term. Things like an oil embargo, or even changes in people's living habits, can drastically affect the bottom line. "There's always a little risk going on in this business," said Norman. "So it's important to look at things over the long term. That's why I never put pressure on our people to meet or change quarter-to-quarter numbers. Most of the financial people would whine about those numbers. But I always stressed the quality of our product, our service, and our execution."

~

IN THE MID-1970S, Norman noticed another trend emerging. Single young people with a high rate of mobility were leading a more free and open lifestyle. "Try as we might, we just couldn't bend Steak & Ale to fill that niche," said Norm. "So, we came up with a new idea."

Norm had always liked the concept of TGI Friday's. He decided to create something similar, but more family- and food-oriented with a lighter menu. Norman also preferred to stay away from the heavy-drinking aspect of the restaurant business. In addition, the new concept would always be open for lunch–which filled a market as only a portion of Steak & Ale restaurants served lunch at the time. Carl Hays, then vice president of operations, recalled that Norman's team "walked around the Friday's bar," and took a good look.

"We had a building in Atlanta that was earmarked to be a Steak & Ale," said Norm. "But, instead, we decided to put the first new restaurant there." The team thought of Irish and Scottish names that would be easy to remember. And in 1976, the first Bennigan's Tavern opened. A short time earlier, Norman had also created the position of director of marketing, and Ron McDougall, who was a successful brand manager for Pillsbury, was recruited for the position and played a major role in the company's eventual success.

Bennigan's quickly became famous for its "Fern Bar," which simply referred to all the plants placed around the bar to make it feel congenial and more like home. And just like Steak & Ale, Bennigan's had a dazzling opening. It was what the people wanted. It filled that other small niche that Norman had observed. Now he had a second chain—one that would eventually grow faster than the first.

Bennigan's growth was also spurred on by leveraging assets through franchising operations and negotiating joint ventures—just as had been done for the Steak & Ale units. Carl Hays was always amazed at Norman's skill at negotiation. "We once had a franchisee who wanted us to buy him out because he needed the money," said Hays. "Norman immediately made a very good offer in order to help the guy out. But the fellow said that the offer wasn't good enough and asked for more money. Then Norman simply said: 'Well, now the offer is for a million dollars less. And the next time you counter, it's going down again.' The franchisee immediately accepted the offer as it stood—one million dollars less than Norman had offered him just a few minutes prior. That Brinker—he was a helluva horse trader!"

∽

AT THIS POINT IN HIS CAREER, Norman had mastered the operations end of the restaurant business (real estate, marketing, finance, personnel, and customer service) and began to focus strategically on managing a large corporation. "My idea of management goes beyond dealing with operations," he said. "It involves working with people to achieve your vision—and make it stronger."

Norm was convinced that in order for people to achieve great things, they had to have high energy levels, passion, and be in good physical condition. So, Steak & Ale encouraged people to join Ken Cooper's Aerobic Center (a few blocks away) by offering to pay half of the entire cost each year. "In a very short time," he recalled, "we had more than three hundred people involved in heavy running. And you could feel the energy level of the company pick up."

Brinker's overall style never involved being heavy-handed. Rather, he tried to work with others by convincing them of the value of his vision. "I wanted to get people to commit to an idea by being personally involved at the outset," he said, "so they could run with it themselves, rather than have me tell them to get something done." That was a lesson he had learned long ago while student body president at San Diego State. And it was a technique that did not go unnoticed by his employees.

"I remember being in a meeting one day," recalled former Steak & Ale supervisor Gary Link, "when Norman popped his head in the door and asked: 'Is it okay if I come in?' Well, what were we going to say, 'no?' So we said, 'Sure, come on in, Norman.' And he sat down and just listened. After awhile, he started asking questions—and then he left! He did that all the time. At first, it annoyed us, but then as time went by, we realized that he was really giving us a lot to think about without taking over and running the meeting. We really respected him for that," recalled Link.

Carl Hays, Steak & Ale's vice president of operations, remembered that Norman came to the realization that he couldn't do everything himself, so he delegated responsibility and authority. "He wasn't always looking over your shoulder," said Hays. "And Norman's priorities very seldom got out of perspective. He knew that Steak & Ale was not going to change the course of human events. So he let us take risks. And when we made mistakes, Norman not only accepted the blame, he was the first guy there to bail us out. 'Gee,' he'd say, '*We* could have done this better,' or '*We* could have done that better.' It was '*we*' rather than '*you.*' With Brinker, it was always a team effort."

Just as Norman was beginning to develop his management/leadership philosophy more fully, he met a fascinating individual at a Young President's Organization (YPO) meeting in Hong Kong. "It was 1976," remembered Norman, "and this man magnified what Nunn and Peterson had said to me years before. I liked him immediately. His name was Stephen Covey."

Shortly after that initial meeting, Norm planned a conference with all Steak & Ale managers in Aspen, Colorado, at which he was anxious to have Covey speak. "I simply felt that his principles of leadership were something that we all needed to hear and learn from," he told one of his associates.

Norman's secretary subsequently called Covey's offices in Utah, but was informed that, due to a prior commitment, he would be unable to attend the conference. "Oh, that won't do," thought Norm. So he picked up the phone himself and called back. "When Covey's secretary answered the phone, I said I wanted to speak to Stephen about coming to this meeting," said Norm. "But, she said, 'I'm sorry, Mr. Brinker, but there's just no way he can make it.'

"Well," replied Norman, "I met him, and I think what he has to say is absolutely right on. So please tell Stephen Covey that he can either come speak on Thursday night, or Friday morning, or Friday afternoon. I have the flight schedules for him to choose from. And, of course, we'll put him up at our expense and pay his fee. Whatever is fair.

"Or else," continued Norm, "on Saturday morning, a Greyhound bus with one hundred people will show up in front of his house to hear what he has to say. Please give him that message for me."

Covey called Norman back later that day and told him he'd be at the Steak & Ale Conference on Friday afternoon. "After that, we formed a close personal relationship," said Norman, "and he's had a major impact on my personal philosophy. Covey's book, *The Seven Habits of Highly Successful People,* came out many years later and is a true masterpiece."

Norm also learned something about leadership from his mother–who walked up to him one day and asked him very simply: "Norman, what are you doing?"

"Well," he replied, "I'm building a lot of new restaurants, and things are really moving."

"No, no, no," said Kathryn with a bit of irritation in her voice. "What else are you doing? What are you doing for your church, for your city, and country? How involved politically are you?"

When he mentioned that he hadn't done very much because he was so busy, Kathryn responded: "You've got to do better than that, Norman! If you don't get involved with others to keep our community on track, it will gradually deteriorate. And if that happens, you will be partly accountable."

Not long after their conversation, Norm hired Rick Berman, an expert in government affairs. Almost immediately, Rick formed for Steak & Ale one of the largest Political Action Committees (PAC) in the United States. Its credo was to support efforts that would help this country's dynamic growth and to create new jobs.

At the very next corporate managers' conference, Norman spoke in some detail on the subject. "I'm not going to talk to you about sales or direction," he told the group. "I'm going to discuss the one thing that can upend us—and that's the federal government. They have no idea of how to create jobs or opportunity. If we're not careful, we'll be out of business thanks to our own government. So, let's focus this meeting on staying in tune with political developments." Fully 90 percent of Steak & Ale's management team participated in the PAC.

Norman also became involved with the Dallas Symphony, the Museum of Art, the Opera, and the Salvation Army. He established a philanthropic trust that contributed to higher education and medical research.

"My mother was right," Norm would later comment. "Being active in your community, taking a stand politically, and giving something back—is all part of the 'caring' aspect of leadership. I should have started much earlier." By his example, Norm Brinker showed that a leader could be both successful in business and also care about people and the world around him.

About this time, Norman became interested in taking a new direction with his life. Now that he had been successful at building an enterprise from scratch, he began to wonder if his leadership style would work in a large conglomerate as well as a small company like Steak & Ale.

In 1976, ten years after the founding of Steak & Ale, Norman's original investment of $5,500 generated more than $103 million in annual sales. It had been a remarkable ride–and he was proud of it. "I became more and more curious about large corporations and their inner workings," he remembered. "As a result, I began to think seriously about merging with a larger organization–but I didn't know which one it should be."

He also felt strongly that such a move might ensure the long-term security of his enterprise and his employees. "I don't worry so much about the idea of going up–as I dread the thought of going down," Norman said. "So, I've always been sure that I didn't risk the company I had built up. That's why I have consistently run things somewhat conservatively."

At this point in his life, Norman began to feel restless with the success he had attained. It was the same feeling he'd experienced when he realized that Brink's Coffee Shop wasn't going where he wanted it to go.

With Brink's, he was restless because of possible failure; with Steak & Ale, he became restless due to success. Whatever the reason, he now realized it was time to wake up and dream new dreams.

◯∕

AGAIN, NORMAN TURNED TO POLO. In the Dallas area, poloists mostly had to play on open-ended fields out in the middle of nowhere. But Norm decided the sport and the

Dallas metroplex needed something better: "I finally found some great property north of town. It was an old turkey farm, but the owners told me it had just been sold to a fellow named Daniel Rabinowitz."

So Norman went to see Rabinowitz and told him that he wanted to buy half of the property and build a world-class polo facility. "Gosh, that sounds like fun," Danny replied. "I'd like to go in on it with you."

So, in a relatively short period of time, the Willow Bend Polo and Hunt Club was founded in Plano, Texas. It included several professionally built polo fields, a hunter's course, a swimming pool, a restaurant, tennis courts, stables for the horses, and shaded grandstands. What's more, Brinker and Rabinowitz began to place advertisements in local newspapers and sell tickets, just as for any other spectator sport.

Now Norman had a place to play polo and hone his athletic skills. By 1976, he was rated a three-goal poloist, which was in the top 5 percent of amateur players. "At one time, I had really hoped to be a five," said Norman. "But I just never could put the amount of time needed into it."

Still, Norm Brinker played regularly, traveled throughout the world participating in exhibitions—and served a four-year term as chairman of the United States Polo Association. His overriding yearly goal was to win the National Silver Cup—which Willow Bend was hosting, and for which he constantly practiced and prepared.

In the fall of 1976, competition for the cup was particularly fierce. Norman's team had advanced to the finals, and they decided to have a Saturday practice round prior to the big game on Sunday. The practice turned out to be unusually fast-paced. At one point, as he aggressively turned to go after a ball that rifled past him, another rider galloping at full speed slammed into the back left side of Norman's mount.

"The horse's head hit me square in the back," he recalled, "and knocked me out of the saddle. When I landed on the ground, I felt this terrible pain in my back—and I couldn't move my legs."

Emergency medical personnel rushed to transport Norman to the nearest hospital. During the ride, he began to hyperventilate, and the medics, suspecting a collapsed lung, administered oxygen. Norman, who was conscious throughout the ordeal, remembered writhing in pain as the ambulance crawled through traffic going to the Texas-Oklahoma football game at the Cotton Bowl. "It just took us forever to get to the hospital," he recalled.

When they arrived at the emergency room, Norm was in such pain that the doctors became concerned about the possibility of internal bleeding. So, without anesthesia, they shoved a needle into his stomach to determine the extent of bleeding. "Boy, the pain in my back was nothing compared to that needle," he remembered. The doctors then noticed that both his liver and spleen had stopped functioning. Internal bleeding, however, did not seem to be a problem.

Subsequent tests revealed that Norman had suffered a collapsed lung, severe trauma causing paralysis to the liver and spleen, two broken ribs, and a dislocated vertebrae in the lower back. The lung, spleen, and liver stabilized rather quickly, but attending physicians were extremely concerned about the dislocated vertebrae. There was a good chance, they told their patient, that he might never again walk upright or without a significant limp.

Norman couldn't believe that the doctors made that kind of a prognosis. "I just knew they were wrong," he remembered. "I really felt like I was going to be okay." And, indeed, Norm would be back walking nicely within a few months and eventually make a complete recovery.

As he settled down alone in his hospital room for what turned out to be a six-night stay, Norman Brinker couldn't seem to fall asleep. Already feeling better, he was actually more annoyed than anything else. After all, he was going to miss the Silver Cup final *and* be out of work for up to a week.

"I just laid there staring at the ceiling," he recalled. "Stayed awake all night."

BRINKER PRINCIPLES

- Try not to micromanage your enterprise.
- Go out and speak to people in person.
- Answer all questions openly and try to help every person who wants to learn.
- Create and maintain a culture that is "can-do," enthusiastic, and enjoyable.
- The foundation of your organization's culture must always be high ethical behavior.
- Allow people to be casual in dress and conversation.
- Give people the freedom to try out their own ideas—even if it means that they fail a time or two.
- Share the wealth. Make people feel they are true partners.
- If you inspire people to commit to an idea, they will run with it on their own.
- Stress the quality of your products and services rather than putting on the pressure to make quarter-to-quarter numbers.
- Give something back. Be active in your community and take a stand politically.
- Run your business conservatively.

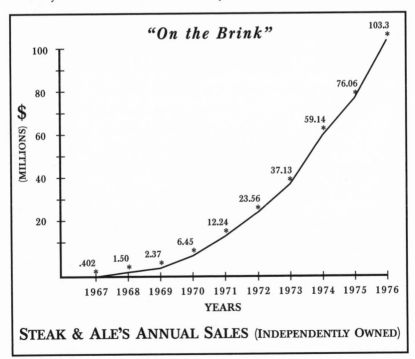

STEAK & ALE'S ANNUAL SALES (INDEPENDENTLY OWNED)

CHAPTER

7.

"Norman, they're going to put a hole in your throat tomorrow, and you're not going to like it. And I just have to tell you that I'm selling all the polo ponies, the ranch, and everything that goes with it. So you'd better wake up...please wake up."

NANCY BRINKER
to Norman, the afternoon of February 6, 1993

"Oh, good morning, Ray."

NORMAN BRINKER,
*the next morning, in response
to Ray Martinez's standard greeting:
"Good morning, Norman"*

The Awakening

At 9:30 A.M. on February 3, 1993, the physician-on-duty walked into St. Mary's intensive care unit to give Norman Brinker his regular morning checkup. Ten minutes later a nurse knocked on the door of the upstairs hospital suite where Nancy Brinker and Margaret Valentine were on the telephones responding to calls that had flooded into the hospital.

"They couldn't get through because your phones were busy," said the nurse. "You're wanted down in intensive care—*now*."

"Oh my God! What's happened to Norman?" Nancy responded.

"They didn't tell me—just get down there."

Nancy and Margaret instinctively ran down the five flights of stairs, because "our adrenaline was rushing too fast to wait for the elevator." The two women arrived to find a crowd gathered around Norman's bed. "It seemed as though every nurse and attendant at the hospital was in that little room," recalled Margaret. "They were packed in two-and three-deep. When I saw them all, I thought Norman had died."

"Come on over here," said the doctor, "there's something I want you to see."

As they moved close to the bed, the doctor took Norman's right hand and addressed his patient: "Mr. Brinker, move your hand, please."

After a momentary delay, Norman slowly flexed the fingers in his hand to make a fist. With that, the people in the room spontaneously erupted into cheers and applause.

Nancy gasped and then clasped her hands in front of her face as tears rolled down her cheeks. Margaret screamed in celebration.

But the smiling doctor made sure to caution everyone: "Now, let's remember that he's still in a coma. This is the first time he has responded to a verbal command. It's a sign that he may be coming out of it. Mr. Brinker has really made a huge turn."

Margaret and Nancy knew instantly that the reaction of the medical people meant more than just a momentary euphoria. "They see so much and bond with so many people," said Margaret, "that they really understood what this step meant. They thought this patient really had a chance to make it; that Norman was in there trying to get out."

The exultation was short-lived, however, because for the next several days there was no progress at all. Nancy would frequently talk to Norman and ask him to squeeze her hand. Sometimes he would respond, sometimes he would not. So everyone fell back into their normal routine, playing classical music, massaging his arms and legs, and talking to him as though he were awake.

On Saturday afternoon, February 6, the doctors conferred with each other and then met with Nancy. They informed her that unless Norman woke up, they planned to perform a tracheotomy the next day, because the tube in his throat would begin to cause permanent damage to his vocal cords. This meant, quite simply, that the doctors had to make an incision at the base of his neck to insert the connection to the mechanical respirator. In comatose patients, this was a process that was usually performed within ten

Kathryn Brinker with son Norman, 1931

Eugene Brinker, Norman's father

Family portrait, early 1940s in Roswell, N.M. Norman's horse, Silver,
is to the right

Norman with first pet rabbit

Norman as a boy of seven

Jumping with Loulee, mother of Injun Joe, at International Jumping Team try-outs in 1949

Norman, far right, with U.S. Olympic Equestrian Team, 1952

Norman, International Equestrian Team, 1949

In the navy, 1952

Norman's horse stumbles on Jump No. 25, Modern Pentathlon Games in Budapest, 1954

Holding onto reins as horse falls on Jump No. 25. Norman breaks shoulder, still manages to finish eighth in a field of sixty riders, 1954

Maureen Connolly Brinker and Norman pursuing favorite pastime, 1952

Norman and Maureen Connolly at opening of Brink's Coffee Shop, 1964

The First Steak & Ale in Dallas, 1966

Just after hitting a shot at a full 30 miles-an-hour gallop

Norman,
just before
a match

Injured restaurant tycoon gets help from friend Perot

By DAVID HOLMBERG
and MARY JANE FINE
Palm Beach Post Staff Writers

WEST PALM BEACH — Back home in Texas, Norman Brinker's friends include Ross Perot and George Bush.

But the influential restaurant tycoon and passionate polo player is also popular in his second home in Wellington.

"Everybody likes him," said Ken Adams, a board member of the South Florida Water Management District and a friend of Brinker's for 10 years. "He's a super guy — very well re-

Perot

spected for his business accomplishments."

Brinker's friends here and in Texas were still watchful and worried Saturday: the 61-year-old multimillionaire remained in stable condition in the intensive care unit of St. Mary's Hospital after an accident during a polo match Thursday in Wellington.

A woman who answered the phone at Brinker's Palm Beach Polo and Country Club home Saturday night said Brinker was "stable and improving," but did not know whether he had regained consciousness.

According to the *Dallas Morning News,* Brinker suffered trauma to the brain stem and broken ribs, but the newspaper quoted sources as saying there was no swelling of the brain, and vital signs were good.

Please see PEROT/4B

Palm Beach Post, January 25, 1993

Brinker Chief Is Injured In Polo Match

By THOMAS C. HAYES

Special to The New York Times

DALLAS, Jan. 24 — Norman E. Brinker, chairman and chief executive of the rapidly growing restaurant company that owns Chili's, remained in stable condition today, apparently still unconscious, three days after a jarring collision during a polo match

The New York Times, January 24, 1993

Brinker International's Chief Is Unconscious After Polo Accident

By a WALL STREET JOURNAL Staff Reporter

DALLAS — Restaurateur Norman Brinker remained hospitalized in stable condition after suffering a head injury in a Florida polo accident last week, but hasn't yet regained consciousness.

The 61-year-old chairman and chief executive officer of **Brinker International** Inc. suffered a "closed head injury"— meaning the skull wasn't penetrated — after his horse and another collided during a match Thursday at the Palm Beach Polo Club, according to Dallas neurosurgeon

Wall Street Journal, January 25, 1993

Brinker Chief Returns to Job 4 Months After Polo Injury

DALLAS, April 4 (Reuters) — The head of the Chili's restaurant chain returned to work today, some four months after suffering a serious head injury while playing polo.

While Mr. Brinker was recovering from the accident that injured his brain stem, he was replaced by Ron McDougall. Today, Mr. McDougall returned to his post as president and

The New York Times, May 5, 1993

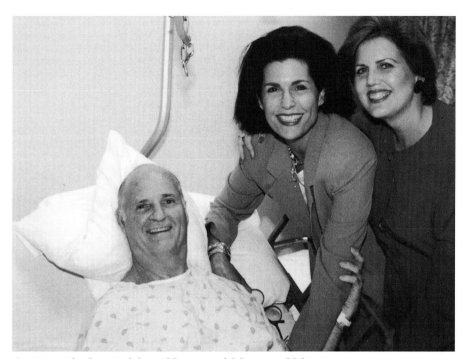

A visit in the hospital from Nancy and Margaret Valentine

Photo given by Ross Perot to Norman while he was still in the coma. Inscription: "Dear Norm. In your absence, *somebody* has to keep morale high with all these beautiful women. As you know, I *hate* this sort of thing, but I am your friend, and I will do it for you. I'm a poor substitute, so please hurry back." Ross

Nancy and Norman, 1995

Dr. Phil Williams

Norman with physical therapists
Robin Stephens Budine and Erin Fay
Azzato, right

Nancy's mom and dad, Ellie and
Marvin Goodman

Norman with speech-language
pathologist Shani Unterhalter
Romick

Norman Brinker

days of the initial onset of the coma. In Norman's case, they had already waited fourteen days.

Immediately after the medical conference, Nancy went into Norman's room and sat down next to his bed. After sitting quietly for a few minutes, she put her hand on her husband's arm and spoke directly into his right ear: "Norman," she said, "they're going to put a hole in your throat tomorrow, and you're not going to like it. And I just have to tell you that I'm selling all the polo ponies, the ranch, and everything that goes with it. So you'd better wake up...please wake up."

Nancy later recalled that when she looked for a reaction, "Norman didn't even twitch. Not a single movement," she said. "I was so dejected."

∽

THE NEXT MORNING, Nancy walked into the room bright and early, and, as usual, started speaking to Norman about how pretty the morning was. Then she sat in the chair to the left of his bed and turned on CNN so that he could hear the early news.

The nurses came in, took their patient's temperature and blood pressure, dressed him, and then left. About a half hour later, the staff doctor arrived and gave Norman his morning checkup. No response, no change. "Looks like the surgical procedure will be done after lunch, Mrs. Brinker," said the doctor as he left.

At 9 A.M. when visiting hours began, family friend Ray Martinez came into the room to spend some time talking about polo—just as he did nearly every morning at Nancy's request. Ray did not expect to hear a response when he gave his customary greeting: "Good morning, Norman."

"Oh, good morning, Ray," said Norman in a muffled voice caused by the tube in his throat.

Ray stopped in his tracks as he was walking across the room; Nancy did a quick double take; and both ceased all motion and stared at Norman for about ten seconds as if paused on a videotape.

Finally, he moved his right arm and turned his head. Nancy started to cry and leaned over him. "Norman, I'm so glad you're awake," she said. "I'm so glad you're here."

With a familiar twinkle in his eyes, Norm smiled and began mumbling. "Don't try to talk," said Nancy. "Just squeeze my hand if you understand me."

Norman squeezed her hand tightly and would not let go.

It was a tender and magic moment.

❧

DR. WILLIAMS FLEW IN FROM DALLAS, and he, along with the local physicians, began a complete physical examination. They found Norman to be totally paralyzed on the left side of his body. In addition, he was thin and gaunt—having lost twenty-five to thirty pounds while in the coma. But he *was* awake and *out* of the coma. The doctors took the tube out of his throat, shut off the mechanical respirator, and abandoned their plans for that afternoon's tracheotomy. Then they moved him out of intensive care into a step-down unit.

Over the next several days, Norman would drift in and out of sleep without saying much in his waking moments. Gradually, though, he began to speak. "When he started talking, he wouldn't make any sense," recalled daughter Brenda. "It was gibberish—but it was fluid and it was incessant."

In a short period of time, the fog lifted, and he was able to identify people easily. And, while he knew *who* he was, he had no idea *where* he was or *what* had happened to him.

Initially, Norm's mind bounced back and forth over a thirty- or thirty-five-year time span—and often slipped back into his childhood. "Gosh! What am I going to do about those darned rabbits," he was heard to mutter over and over again.

When the doctors asked him where he was, Norman responded: "I'm on a boat in San Diego."

"Where do you work?" they inquired. "At Jack-In-The-Box and Steak & Ale," he answered.

And when one of the doctors held a mirror in front of him and asked him who he saw, Norman replied: "An old man."

"It was kind of sad," recalled the doctor, "but not at all an unusual response for a patient with his injury."

Another common symptom Norm experienced for a time was an inability to distinguish day from night. The hypothalamus gland, which regulates a person's biological clock, had also been affected. "But that condition will pass within a few weeks," the doctors assured Nancy.

While Norman experienced an early short-term loss of memory and remembered absolutely nothing about the accident, he seemed to have no real speech problems, such as slurring words or stuttering. He did, however, sometimes mistake Nancy for his mother, Kathryn. "Norman had always told me that I reminded him of his mother in a lot of ways," said Nancy. "But when he began to call me Kathryn, I couldn't help but wonder if my playing the classical music over the last several weeks had anything to do with it."

One problem Norm experienced in the early going was that he simply could not be still. He began bucking, thrashing, and kicking on his right side—almost uncontrollably. "He was in a state of perpetual motion," recalled Margaret. "But, to tell you the truth, that was almost normal for Norman. Before the accident, he literally trotted everywhere he went."

The doctors and nurses were forced to strap him in the bed when he sat up because of that constant motion. Eric recalled once walking into the hospital room to see his dad restrained with leather belts. "Hey Eric," said Norman, "good to see you. How're you doing? Come over here and undo this darned harness, will you?"

"Well, I don't know, Dad. Don't the doctors want it on?"

"Oh, it's okay. I just can't stand to be tied down."

So Eric went over to the bed and untied his father. "The next thing I knew, Dad almost fell out of bed from his active motion," said Eric. "After that, we strapped him in again."

While he was tied down, the family brought in a video recorder and ran some family home movies and new-release motion pictures. But Norman wouldn't pay any attention to those tapes. He'd look around the room and continue to talk and thrash back and forth.

One day, however, Nancy, put in a video of one of his polo matches. "All of a sudden," she remembered, "Norman calmed down. He focused on the film. He didn't thrash at all, and he didn't talk. The polo tapes had an amazing effect on him."

Polo, and horses in particular, had always been Norman's passion in life. He took to the sport as if born to it, and it helped relieve stress in his business and professional life. Now, it had a calming, soothing effect on him during a time when he was his most vulnerable, raw, innate self.

When she saw how Norm reacted, Nancy asked George Olivas to view the polo tapes with Norman. And whenever George showed up, Norm's mind was not in some past memory—he was focused on the present—and he had a normal conversation. "Hi, George," Norman would say. "Tell me, what's the status of the horses? How are they all doing?"

"He remembered all the names of the horses," George would recall. "And he could describe the details of some of our past polo matches. It was amazing to me how much he remembered."

Norman was also extraordinarily sincere in expressing his thoughts and emotions. As a matter of fact, he was *brutally* honest in his conversations with family members. "He lectured us all on our faults," remembered Cindy. "Some of us were too hyper, some insecure, some unfocused, and some out of shape. Basically, he told us all the things he was usually too nice to say. He let everybody have it."

Interestingly enough, Norman's frankness presented a minor problem that his son, Eric, tried to solve. Norm came out of his coma exactly one week before his and Nancy's twelfth wedding anniversary—which was on February 14, Valentine's Day.

Eric bought balloons and a present for Norman to give to Nancy. He asked the nurse to sign the card, "Love, Norman." And then he coached Norman all morning on what to say.

"Now, Dad, what are you going to say to Mom?" Eric asked.

"Well, I'm going to tell her she's talking too much," he replied.

"No, Dad, no. You can't tell her that. You've got to tell her 'Happy Anniversary.'"

"Okay," said Norman.

"Okay, Dad. What are you going to say to her?"

"Well, I'm going to tell her to calm down—that she's too high-strung."

"No, Dad, no. You've got to tell her 'Happy Anniversary.'"

Later that morning, when Nancy walked into the room, Norman held out the present and card and said: "Happy Anniversary, honey!"

"Mom was so overcome. She couldn't say anything," remembered Eric. "She just started crying and hugging Dad."

When Dr. Phil Williams heard that story later in the day, he quipped: "It's a good thing Norman woke up before February 14, or he'd have had a *real* head injury–this one inflicted by Nancy."

∼

ON THEIR ANNIVERSARY, Nancy brought in several newspaper articles that had been written about the accident. One clipping in *The Wall Street Journal,* for example, reported that Norm Brinker's injury had generated more queries than any other injury they'd ever reported, with the exception of the assassination attempt on President Reagan.

Publicity like that generated thousands of cards, notes, and faxes sent by people to Norman from all over the world; some from people who hadn't seen him in forty years; some from people he didn't know at all. Many of the letters were up to eight pages long and wrote about the upbeat effect he had on their lives. All of them wished him a speedy recovery in touching terms.

Norman was moved by the outpouring of affection. "I think it was then that I first resolved to get better quickly," he said. "It really meant a lot to me that so many people cared. I wanted to get better for them. I wanted to get better for my family. And I wanted to do it for myself. I remember thinking that I just *had* to get rid of those straps and stand up on my own."

Norman's energy level was now increasing with each day. Not only was he getting stronger physically in his arms and legs, but he also was rapidly recovering from his head injury. Doctors, however, told him that, due to the grave extent of his injuries and subsequent paralysis, it would take at least a year or more to realize any kind of a meaningful recovery.

"I told them they were wrong," said Norman. "Absolutely wrong."

8

"I don't have any plans for you. Do you think I would come here and belittle you that way? No, not at all. I hope that we will develop a plan—together.

NORMAN BRINKER,
to officers of Burger King,
upon assuming the chairmanship

"In the beginning, we weren't sure that we could turn Burger King around. But after we got things moving in the right direction, there was no more uncertainty. And for me, when you take all the risk out, it just isn't as much fun."

NORMAN BRINKER,
on his time as chairman of Burger King

Pillsbury and Burger King

While searching for new Steak & Ale restaurant locations in Oklahoma City, Norman accepted an offer to give a speech to the Oklahoma Restaurant Association. There he happened to run into Jim McLamore, the founder of Burger King and a member of the board of directors of the Pillsbury Corporation, its parent company.

In a casual conversation, Norm mentioned to Jim that he was interested in placing Steak & Ale with a larger company that was also interested in the restaurant business. "I've asked Goldman Sachs to be on the lookout for us," he told McLamore, "but they only have about ten companies on the list that we would consider at all." Pillsbury was not one of them, because, at the time, the company owned a wholesale wine business that prevented it from legally owning a restaurant chain that served alcoholic beverages.

"Well, as a matter of fact," said McLamore, "the Pillsbury board has been considering selling the wine business. Let me find out the status, and I'll get back to you." Two days later, Bill Spoor, chairman of the Pillsbury Corporation, was on the phone to Norman indicating a strong interest in Steak & Ale.

The time was right for a major move, Norm believed. He saw Steak & Ale as a vibrant company that was one-dimensional—steak-oriented only. A merger, he believed, would offer his employees more opportunity to pursue different avenues in their careers. It would also give him a chance to do something different, learn more, and grow professionally. Another compelling reason for such a move was that Norman's partner desired to liquidate his percentage of the business.

So, when Pillsbury's Bill Spoor called, the timing was right for a deal. Steak & Ale subsequently merged with Pillsbury when Spoor agreed to purchase all outstanding shares for eighteen dollars each—a total of $102 million for 102 Steak & Ale restaurants. "Not bad," Norman thought at the time, "a million dollars a restaurant."

As a result, Norm Brinker became an executive vice president with Pillsbury, and subsequently chairman of S & A (newly named division that included Steak & Ale and Bennigan's)—and the largest individual holder of Pillsbury stock. He had successfully negotiated one of the most lucrative mergers in the history of the restaurant business up to that time.

Initially, Norm's intentions were to stay with Pillsbury only long enough to make sure that the company got what it paid for. And he wanted to be certain that his team was treated well. But the longer he stayed involved, the more Norman found the environment to be vibrant and stimulating. "I decided to stay on with Pillsbury," he said, "and during the next several years, we were able to develop the Bennigan's concept into more than 150 units. And Steak & Ale just kept on growing. It was a wonderfully fun time."

～

IN APRIL OF 1980, Norman was in Morocco on a Young President's Organization trip when he received a call from Dallas. His mother, Kathryn, who had recently moved to a retirement community, suddenly had become very ill and was holding on to see him again. Norm was told he needed to return home immediately.

On the long plane ride back home, Norman thought about his mother and her life. He remembered her planning every day of her only son's early life to be certain that he had what was needed in the form of emotional support and sustenance. He remembered that she kept the house, cooked, and cleaned; that she got a job at a bakery when times were tough; and that she moved to Dallas for him when Maureen died.

He remembered that she would call her friends all around the country so as to stay in touch; and of her once telling the *Dallas Morning News*: "When Norman was a little boy and into all those shenanigans, I always knew he would turn out to be a dynamic man–if I could just live through his childhood."

And he remembered Kathryn saying: "Norman, you've got to listen to opera so you'll be rounded"; and "Norman, you've got to always do better–and then be certain you give a significant amount of time to your community, country, and church." If it hadn't been for her, he knew he wouldn't be where he was today. He wouldn't have nearly the appreciation he had for people–or for life itself. And Norm also realized from whom a lot of his determination and zest for life came.

"Mother had told me a number of times in 1978 and 1979 that she was ready to go," Norman recalled. "She said that she had some exciting things she wanted to do, but that her body just couldn't keep up with her mind. 'It's just a real struggle,' she told me. 'I'm ready to move on and go into the next life. It will be wonderful.'"

Kathryn Brinker died peacefully in her sleep on April 18, 1980. She was seventy-eight years old. Her son was at her bedside.

∼

ABOUT EIGHTEEN MONTHS LATER, Norman was at LaGuardia Airport preparing to return home from a restaurant opening in New York. His plane was canceled because of equipment failure–so he sprinted back into the terminal and quickly boarded another jet headed for Dallas.

As he walked down the aisle, Norman noticed an open seat next to a friend of his. But with a lot of work to do during the flight, he said hello and then went to the back of the plane. "A half hour before we landed, I went up front and sat down next to Selly Belofsky to chat," said Norm. "He brought up the name of a woman he had introduced me to at a social function a year earlier."

"Why don't you call Nancy Goodman and ask her to lunch," urged Selly. "I know she's not involved with anyone, and, besides, I think you two would like each other very much."

So when Norman returned to Dallas, he called Nancy and asked her to lunch. "Is this the person who walks on water?" Norman jested.

"Who is this?" she said at first. "Just kidding, Norm. I would like that very much."

The two hit it off right away. "I was attracted to her vitality and her excitement," said Norman. "She was also as bright as she could be. She reminded me of Kathryn with her sense of direction, her sense of fulfillment, and her desire to do things for others."

And Nancy, too, had immediate and strong feelings for Norman. "I had never met anyone like him," she said. "He was that dynamic Roy-Rogers-kind-of-guy I had always dreamed of meeting. He whirled me off my feet."

Four months later, Norman and Nancy surprised all their friends and family by getting married—on Valentines Day, 1981.

∼

AFTER SIX YEARS OF REMARKABLE GROWTH for S & A, Norman Brinker was named president of the Pillsbury Restaurant Group in March of 1982. His new responsibilities included overseeing not only Steak & Ale and Bennigan's, but Poppin' Fresh restaurants and Burger King. He was now in charge of the second-largest restaurant company in the world, with approximately 150,000 employees and more than $3.5 billion in annual sales.

One of the main reasons for Norman's promotion was the fact that Burger King, the second-largest fast-food chain in the world, with 3,300 units, had begun to falter operationally. Chairman Bill Spoor believed it needed a renewal–and that Brinker was just the person to provide it and get excitement back in the company.

At first, Norm balked at assuming both the chairmanship and presidency of Burger King. "They wanted to move me to Minneapolis," he recalled, "but I liked Dallas too much to leave." Spoor, however, readily agreed to support Norman.

"Bill was great," said Norm. "He told me to go ahead and live in Dallas and travel back and forth to Miami (Burger King headquarters) when I needed to be there. 'Either place,' he said, 'you're at home.'"

While Norman had responsibility for all of Pillsbury's restaurants, it was clear that he would have to spend most of his time working to bring Burger King back to prominence. Through his top executives, to whom he delegated authority, Norm maintained oversight responsibility of the other restaurants, which were already doing quite well. Basically, he made sure each chain was still growing at an acceptable rate by exceeding customer needs and delivering a very pleasant experience at a reasonable price.

At the same time, he took a hands-on approach in Miami and set out to employ the management style he had developed and see if it worked in a very large company that had been around for years. "My first thoughts were to get the right people in the right places and then establish an atmosphere that encouraged everyone to contribute their best ideas and efforts," said Norman.

"I also wanted to establish 'bottom-up' communication instead of 'top-down,'" he remembered. "I was determined to make business more enjoyable for the Burger King people–more freewheeling, more innovative, and more creative."

Next, Norman went out to the field. During his first thirty days, he visited all ten Burger King regions—traveling to such cities as Phoenix, San Francisco, Miami, New York, and Chicago, among others. He had been cautioned, however, not to meet with certain franchisees who were viewed as disruptive by the home office. Rather than not inviting them, Norman wrote a personal letter of invitation to the disruptive ones. "Dear Jim (or whoever)," he wrote. "I would like to meet with you and Burger King's other supervisors and franchisees in Miami on a certain date. If you find that time inconvenient, please let me know, and we'll change it."

"No one asked to change the date of a meeting," recalled Norman, who met not only with franchisees, but also with supervisors, managers, and employees. He observed operations by walking into restaurants, talking to customers, asking opinions, and generally seeing firsthand what the problems were with the chain.

Some of the frontline managers complained that Burger King management did not listen to them, didn't care, and didn't understand their challenges. Several people, including customers, told him that some of the menu items—specifically the steak sandwich, the chicken sandwich, and the veal parmesan sandwich—were overpriced, crummy, and of poor quality.

So Norman sampled the food himself to see firsthand what the customers and franchisees were talking about. He tasted the veal parmesan sandwich, for instance. "It was really not good," he recalled. "The covered lid tasted better than the sandwich."

From similar expeditions to the field, Norman came up with the idea of allowing customers to get their own drinks. As a result, Burger King put in a drink refill bar, gave customers cups, and they were allowed to get their own drinks and have free refills. The only question remaining was whether or not people would overdrink and cost the company more money. Interestingly enough, the new policy actually saved time and money, because the counter people no longer had to fill up cups–and the amount customers overdrank was negligible.

In an organization like Burger King, Norm Brinker realized that little things–like counter people not filling up cups with ice and cokes–could make a big difference to the bottom line. "In business," he often said, "money saved is truly money earned."

After a couple of weeks in Miami, Norman decided to call a meeting of Burger King's top echelon of officers–all ninety-two of them. That meeting started under quite difficult circumstances for the new chairman and president, who was viewed as something of an outsider to the rest of the executives. "What did Brinker know about fast food?" most of them thought. In addition, half of the group believed they should have been named the new boss, because they had more time with the company.

As Norman entered the room, most of the ninety-two were sitting stern-faced with their arms folded. "It was not a positive sight, to say the least," Norman said. "So, I decided to begin the meeting by inviting them to ask questions to see what was on their minds."

The first person who raised his hand was blunt: "What are your plans for Burger King?" he asked.

Norm's response was quick and firm: "I don't have any plans for you," he said. "Do you think I would come here and belittle you that way? No, not at all. I hope that *we* will develop a plan *together*–and support that plan with 110 percent of our effort.

"But after we do so," continued Norman, "we'll all support it. And if there's any talk about the plan behind anyone's back–then you're gone, *you're gone.* And that has to be crystal clear. On the other hand, if there's anything about the plan we can improve, then don't hesitate to bring it up at the appropriate time in the appropriate setting."

After hearing those opening remarks, people subconsciously began to unfold their arms–indicating they were becoming a bit more receptive. But when Norman said that they should now all discuss "who we are, what we are, and where we're going"–arms began to fold again.

"I knew what they were thinking," he remembered. "They were thinking: 'Yeah, right. We're a company that's twenty-five years old, and now we want to talk about who we are! Give me a break!'"

However, as the group began to start communicating, they filled four big sheets of paper with facts about what Burger King really was. Some of the group said that their company was number two in the industry, that they were fast, and that they served high-quality food. When Norman heard that last claim, he challenged them.

"High quality, huh? What about the steak sandwich? Besides being tough, inconsistent, tasteless, and chewy– it's too expensive," he said. "And how about the chicken sandwich? I'm told it used to be a lot better at five ounces. Now it's nine ounces. And what about the veal parmesan sandwich?"

One of the officers stood up and agreed with Norman. "Yeah, it tastes like a stale cowpattie," he said. And everyone else agreed except the guys from New York, who liked it. "Okay," said Norman, "we'll keep it in New York. But, elsewhere, the veal parmesan sandwich is history."

In general, the meeting turned out to be a wonderful success. The group collectively agreed to simplify things and return to the basics that had previously made Burger King great. They stopped emphasizing oversized chicken, fish, and other specialty sandwiches and, instead, concentrated on hamburger items such as the Whopper. Some stores stayed open longer hours, and others began to offer breakfast. And the company also introduced salad bars in most of their restaurants. "That immediately gave us something of an upscale tint," said Norm.

The last thing he did at the meeting was to challenge the group of ninety-two to think up a way that they could stimulate sales by 10 percent during the coming fiscal year. "That's really all I said to them," remembered Norman. "And you'll never believe what happened after that. The talent and energy that was released was simply amazing."

Jeff Campbell, president of Burger King, and Kyle Craig, executive vice president, had previously come up with an idea called "Battle of the Burgers," which Norman and the other executives heartily endorsed. "I believed it would give the public a clear image of who we were and what we were all about," he said, "not to mention increasing our marketing tempo."

Twice, Burger King commissioned random and independent consumer research projects in various cities across the country. Both times the results were the same: People preferred Burger King hamburgers over McDonald's on a blind taste test. So an advertising agency worked up storyboards and produced commercials about which method of cooking the average person preferred, "broiling or frying."

In August, prior to the launch of the campaign, Norman decided to meet with all of Burger King's franchisees: "The company was nearly 85 percent franchises, and I wanted to be certain they understood the risks involved in the commercials. And besides," said Norm, "if I think of someone as a partner, I darn sure don't want to catch them by surprise or take them for granted."

So, at a major meeting in Chicago, the "Battle of the Burgers" campaign was explained to all the franchisees at once. Their reactions were very enthusiastic, recalled Norman. "I think they were more excited and more positive about these things than we were," he said.

On September 22, less than six months after the first meeting of the ninety-two Burger King officers, television commercials began airing across the country. The campaign so shook up McDonald's that the company immediately filed a suit against Burger King for an injunction against the advertisements, alleging that there were no accurate taste tests that proved people loved broiling over frying. Kyle Craig, Burger King's executive spokesman, also appeared on ABC's *Nightline* to defend his company's position publicly.

The next day, a federal judge refused to grant McDonald's request–and a nationwide "Battle of the Burgers" was on. Across the country people started doing taste tests on television–trying to determine whether Burger King's Whopper was better than McDonald's Big Mac.

Newspapers, magazines, and schools got into the act and sponsored their own taste testing. The publicity went on and on and on. It could not have been better for Burger King's business.

"I never dreamed McDonald's would sue," said Norman. "In fact, I couldn't believe they did. That brought us more attention than we could have ever hoped for."

The effect on sales was nothing less than remarkable. Kyle Craig enthusiastically reported double-digit growth, which lasted for twenty successive months. The company recorded its greatest year-to-year pretax profits increase–and store operating profits as a percentage of business also hit a record high.

All in all, Burger King doubled its earnings from $60 million to $125 million in less than two years.

Norman was also proud of the fact that he had chopped very few jobs. "Too often executives will come in and start axing employees right away. In the end, I only had to terminate three or four people. We moved a lot of people around to make it more interesting for them; and we did shrink the total headquarters office by eighty-five people because there were too many layers of management. But we were very careful to find jobs for them with the company or through outplacement programs. Everything worked out for everybody."

∼

PILLSBURY'S ENTIRE GROUP OF RESTAURANTS was doing extraordinarily well. Steak & Ale and Bennigan's were still number one in their niches, Poppin' Fresh was very profitable, and Burger King was beginning to close the gap on McDonald's. "The trick to managing a large group," Norman said, "is to operate the chains as separate entities, under separate, stable management, with separate styles and ambience."

Part of his philosophy was to place bright, energetic young people in positions of high authority and then work with them in a mentor/student relationship. Norman had elevated two thirty-six-year-olds, Hal Smith and Mike Jenkins, to the chairmanship and presidency of Steak & Ale; and had positioned thirty-nine-year-old Jeff Campbell as head of Burger King. "I've always felt a great deal of satisfaction in being able to give younger executives a hand up the ladder and watch them grow," said Norman. "Few executives in high positions of authority offer to coach and bring others along. I always made time for that—often with outstanding results."

From the outside looking in, many observers have looked at Norm Brinker's business success and remarked that "Brinker was a *lucky* guy." But, in reality, Norman created his own luck. He not only cared about people and helped develop their careers, he also was achievement-oriented. Norman got out there and made things happen. He was also curious, had an open mind, approached his job intelligently and pragmatically—and he was people-oriented. Had he been autocratic in style, he would never have achieved the degree of business success he eventually attained. "It was also fun for me," said Norman. "It's been like a sport. You play by the rules. You're careful. You're imaginative. You're knowledgeable. And you attract, keep, and coach the most talented leaders in the industry. I've always had a wonderful time in the game of restaurant building."

But as his restaurants became more and more successful, Norm became less and less stimulated. Pillsbury was such a large organization that he was unavoidably swamped in bureaucracy—which Norman did not enjoy at all. In addition, he was traveling somewhere between 160,000 and 170,000 miles each year—far too much even for a mover like Brinker.

But more than anything else, Norman began to become impatient again—just as he had after Steak & Ale had reached its peak. "In the beginning, we weren't sure that we could turn Burger King around. But after we got things moving in the right direction, there was no more uncertainty. And for me, when you take all the risk out, it just isn't as much fun."

And therein was a great paradox for Norman Brinker. He enjoyed the excitement involved in creating an entrepreneurial venture—and he had been extraordinarily successful at it. Yet, once victory was achieved, for Norman, the thrill dissipated.

Now his mind began to fill with new thoughts and new dreams. He wondered, for example, if his leadership style would work in a smaller organization that had to compete against the big restaurant chains.

So, Norman went to meet with John Whitehead, a member of the Pillsbury board of directors and chairman of the board of Goldman Sachs. "I told him the challenge was gone," recalled Norman, "and that I really wanted to do something different." Whitehead suggested that Brinker continue with Burger King awhile longer, and then they would begin looking for an exciting new opportunity.

~

ABOUT THAT TIME, Larry Lavine, the owner of a small hamburger chain called Chili's, began serious discussions with S&A about a merger or acquisition. After a final meeting in Minneapolis, the consensus was that the timing wasn't right for an immediate acquisition. Pillsbury was opening a Burger King every day–and a Steak & Ale and Bennigan's once a week. The decision was made to look at Chili's again in eight to twelve months.

At home a few nights later, Norman mentioned to Nancy that he was somewhat disappointed in the final decision, because he thought it would have been a great opportunity. "Well, you don't need to worry about that anymore," she said, "because I read in this evening's newspaper that Larry has made a deal to sell Chili's to Saga Corporation."

Norman could not hide his disappointment at that news. But rather than moping around, his mind began to twist and turn. A few hours later, as Nancy was combing her hair in the bedroom, she noticed a glint in her husband's eyes: "Norman," she said, "why don't you call Larry and see if you can't salvage that deal? As a matter of fact, you could do the deal yourself."

"Well, to tell you the truth," he replied, "I have been thinking about doing just that."

"Well, if that's what you want to do, then do it."

With Nancy's encouragement, Norman went right to the telephone and called Larry Lavine to congratulate him on his merger. During their conversation, Larry mentioned that he had received an offer of $35 million in cash plus $1 million for three years. When Norman told him that he could get a whole lot more if he went public and then asked him why he didn't do that instead, Larry replied honestly: "Because I don't know how."

After a moment's pause, Norman said: "Say, would you like to get together sometime soon?"

"Yes," said Larry. "I'd like to meet with you personally and privately." The following Saturday, Lavine met Brinker at Norman's home to discuss the possibility of Norman buying part of Chili's. "I didn't want to sound like I wanted strong-arm control of the operation, so I offered to purchase 40 percent, " recalled Norm. "After discussing my real desire to get back to building a smaller company with my management strategy, and after a bit of interesting horse trading, Larry was quite excited and felt he could withdraw Chili's pending sale."

The private meeting went very well, and as Lavine left, he said that he needed to talk to his brother, a partner in Chili's, before he made a final decision. "Great," replied Norman. "Why don't you give me a call in a few days and let me know?" Later that same night, Larry called back and said he was ready to go.

Norman and Larry then began clearing the way for their business relationship to come about smoothly. Lavine contacted Saga to tell them that he wasn't going through with the deal. Saga's president then flew to Dallas in an attempt to get him to change his mind. But, in the end, no breach of contract complaint was made.

And Norman went to Pillsbury to make certain that the board wouldn't have a problem with his decision or charge him with a conflict of interest. "I went up to Minneapolis the Monday before the next board meeting to meet with Bill Spoor," Norman remembered. "I wanted to meet with him personally to discuss the matter."

Spoor's reaction was extraordinarily charged: "Norman," he said, "you have all the fun. You're an entrepreneur. I should be an entrepreneur. You're doing what I should be doing. I've been with Pillsbury for thirty-five years—it's not *that* much fun."

When the board met, the members were upset and disappointed with Norman's resignation. But, with both Bill Spoor and John Whitehead voicing support, everybody calmed down and wished him well. "The people at Pillsbury were wonderful to me," said Norm. "It meant very much that we remained friends and colleagues after I left."

With all avenues now clear, Norman Brinker, through his horse trade with Larry Lavine, purchased 40 percent of Chili's on a seven-year note. During the first three years there were no payments of any kind. Starting in year four, interest and principal were equal at 10 percent.

With that, Brinker took over as CEO and chairman while Lavine remained president. Larry gave up a sure $38 million for the chance of going public. But Norman's risk was equally steep.

When he took over in 1983, Chili's was a Dallas-based chain of twenty-three specialty hamburger restaurants doing $35 million in annual sales.

Pillsbury was still the second-largest restaurant corporation in the world, with sales exceeding $3.5 billion yearly. And Norm Brinker was the leading Pillsbury stockholder, making a strong six-figure salary with bonuses.

"I was willing to give it all up for a much lower salary," said Norman, "so that I could start with a new entrepreneurial challenge—where I could be on the front lines again. That's what I really wanted to do."

"By moving to Chili's, I put my reputation on the line again—and there was also the very real danger of a significant monetary loss. Actually, both risks were part of the reason I did it."

∼

ON THE FOURTH OF JULY holiday weekend in 1983, Norman was playing in a polo tournament at Willow Bend. His final match was on Saturday, and the next business day was to be his first day on the job at Chili's. As a matter of fact, he had scheduled an 8 A.M. meeting with Larry Lavine and other top executives.

Norman's daughter, Cindy, was in the grandstand that day to watch her dad play polo. She had asked a friend and his parents to accompany her to the match. "We were all sitting there," Cindy remembered, "when my friend's father tapped me on the shoulder and commented that polo looked kind of dangerous. 'Does your father ever get hurt doing this?' he asked."

Cindy responded that while her dad had taken a couple of falls in the past, he was actually an expert horseman who very rarely got seriously hurt. "As I was speaking over my shoulder to him," said Cindy, "his eyes got bigger and bigger, and I heard some shudders and screams around me. When I turned around, it was obvious that there had been a major accident, and Dad had been thrown off his horse."

This was an accident that Norman would later remember vividly. "I was galloping at full speed right in front of the scoreboard," he recalled. "I went down for a nearside back shot, and another horse's legs hit my horse's front legs—causing my horse to fall. The impact quickly threw me in the air, head over heels, and I landed hard."

Norman was rushed by ambulance to Presbyterian Hospital in Dallas. He was fully conscious but in terrible pain and unable to walk. After a thorough examination, doctors diagnosed a partially shattered pelvis, a broken pelvic bone, torn ligaments across the pelvis, and a couple of broken ribs. "And my back hurt, too," said Norm.

The physicians told him that it would take six to eight weeks to heal and another several months of rehabilitation after that. "It's a very serious injury, Mr. Brinker," said the attending physician. "You've got to take it slow."

But Norman seemed unconcerned about the injuries. His mind, rather, was on Chili's and what he was going to do to make it a success.

With this accident, Norman knew he had to make a quick recovery. "My God!" he thought to himself. "I'm starting a new job on Tuesday. I have a new business to build. I just don't have time to be hurt."

"I was determined to get involved with Chili's immediately—broken bones or no broken bones."

BRINKER PRINCIPLES

....

- Make your business more freewheeling, more innovative, and more creative.
- The first thing you should do in a new business is go out into the field and see for yourself what's going on.
- In a large organization, little things can have a big impact on the bottom line. Money saved is truly money earned.
- Seek to understand before you seek to be understood. Answer questions first.
- Develop plans together with your team. And then allow no one to talk behind anyone else's back.
- Issue a challenge to your best people and then get out of the way and let their collective talent and energy take over.
- When you think of someone as a partner, don't catch them by surprise. Make sure they understand the risks involved.
- Operate different parts of your organization as separate entities, under separate, stable management, with separate styles.
- Place bright, energetic young people in positions of authority and then work with them in a mentor/student relationship.

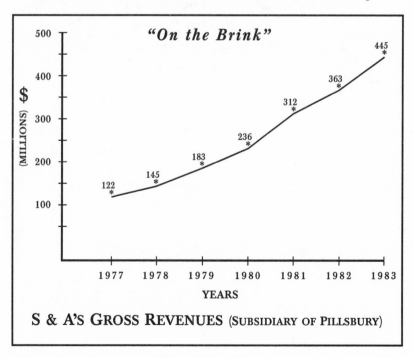

S & A'S GROSS REVENUES (SUBSIDIARY OF PILLSBURY)

9.

*"I've had a lifetime of training and
experiences that got me through this."*

NORMAN BRINKER,
quoted in Fortune magazine, August 15, 1994

*"I've heard what you have to say. Now I
want you to understand me because I know
my body, and I'm paying the bills. I'm
going to be home by May 1—no wheelchair,
no crutches, no cane."*

NORMAN BRINKER,
*to his doctors, who told him it would be a year or two
before he could walk unaided, March 1, 1993*

*"Okay. I'm standing up.
It's a wonderful day."*

NORMAN BRINKER,
March 5, 1993

The Recovery

In late February 1993, about two weeks after awakening from the coma, Norman left St. Mary's and checked into Pinecrest Rehabilitation Hospital in Delray Beach, Florida. After a tour of the facility, where the rules were explained, Nancy pulled the entire staff together for a heart-to-heart.

"Look," she said, "I know that your rules are appropriate for most of your patients, but they won't work for Norman. I want him to have a private room, and I want him surrounded by people who look like his restaurant managers. They need to be perky, young, cute, and fun-loving. Believe me, that's the only way he's going to recover."

"Okay," the staff responded collectively. "That's what we'll do."

Norman's early wooziness had been a serious concern to Nancy, who spoke with the doctors about it. When they said it might be a result of the drug Dilantin, which had been administered since he was in the coma, Nancy inquired why it was still necessary. "Well," responded one physician, "it is a drug often used for patients with a head wound like Norman sustained. Essentially, it controls the seizures that often accompany such an injury."

"Well, since he really hasn't had any problems with seizures, and he's awake now, why don't we take him off of it for a while and see what happens," said Nancy.

The doctors agreed to give it a try as long as the Brinkers signed a consent waiver. Within forty-eight hours, Norman was noticeably more alert and lucid. As a matter of fact, he now asked Nancy the question she had been longing to hear: "How much is all this costing?"

"I just laughed and gave him a big kiss," she recalled. "That's when I knew he'd be okay."

As Norman was able to think with more lucidity, he also became more determined to recover. He constantly sought people to massage and move the left side of his body. When visitors would come into his room, for instance, he'd ask them to lift up his left arm and then drop it down. "I wouldn't know if it was up or down unless I looked," he recalled. "I had absolutely no feeling whatsoever in that part of my body. I was paralyzed with no sense of movement."

More than anything, though, Norman was determined to get out of Pinecrest quickly. He did not like being cooped up and was frustrated by being confined to a wheelchair so much of the time. The family would take him for brief outside walks every day so that he could get some sun. On one occasion, Nancy's mother pulled up in her car, noticed Eric with Norman, and walked up to them.

"Oh, hi, Miss Ellie," said Norman.

"Hi, Norman," she responded. "How are you feeling?"

"Now, Ellie," replied Norm matter-of-factly, "where's your car?"

"Well, it's right over there in the parking lot."

"Okay, let's go," he said. "Take me over there to the car. Load this chair in there. We're getting out of here right now. We're leaving."

"No, Norman," Ellie said with a smile, "you've got to stay here for a while and get better."

"No," he replied, "I'm getting out of here. Bring me a car. I'll drive myself out of here. My *right* arm and leg are working well."

At that moment, Norman spotted the Life-Flight helicopter ambulance sitting on the facility's landing pad. "Hey" he said, "there's a helicopter. Come on, Eric. Get me on that chopper. We're getting out of here!"

∼

EVEN THOUGH NORM WAS FRUSTRATED and wanted to leave, Ellie's words had an impact on him. He *was* going to have to stay at Pinecrest for a while, he thought. And he *was* going to get much better.

It was then that Norman Brinker realized that he had been given a new and different kind of assignment. It had to do with rebuilding himself after he'd been neurologically disassembled. But how? How was he going to do it?

"Well," he reasoned, "let's see if the business philosophy works on a personal basis." So that's what he decided to do—employ the same strategy he had used to lead Steak & Ale and Bennigan's, Pillsbury's, Burger King, and Brinker International's Chili's.

Norman's first step was to begin with the end in mind.

He decided to try to make it home by May 1, 1993, so that he could attend the Brinker International board meeting on May 4. At that time, he would reassume the chairmanship of his company.

The second step was to seek to understand before he sought to be understood. With that, Norm and Nancy asked all the doctors for a complete physical evaluation and prognosis. He was informed in straight talk and plain language that he was paralyzed on the left side of his body, that he'd been through a terrible trauma, and that he would require one to two years of rehabilitation therapy. "You shouldn't plan to be out of Pinecrest before January 1, 1994, at the earliest," the doctors said sternly. "But don't worry, Mr. Brinker, we'll help you get back home."

"I listened to all the doctors," Norman recalled. "And when they didn't have anything more to say, I asked them to clearly understand my intentions."

He began by telling them a story. "Gentlemen," he said, "when I was ten years old, I got ptomaine poisoning while I was on my country paper route. I was so sick, I thought I'd die. So I went to a phone and called my mother, who was working her day job at the bakery. When I told her I was sick and asked her to help me deliver my papers in her car, she said: 'No, I can't do that. I love you very much, and I wish I could help you. But I've got a job here, and I just can't leave. I know this is uncomfortable for you, but that's the way things are when you're uncomfortable. You need to buckle up, Norman,' she said finally, 'and finish your paper route. If you get so sick that you just can't do it at all, then let me know.'

"Well," Norm continued, "I thought if that's the way it's supposed to be done, that's what I'll do. I delivered my papers by riding my bike the final eight miles of gravel roads. Then I went home to rest. And that's what I'm going to do right now. I'm going to buckle up and travel the rough road back home.

"I've heard what you all have to say. Now I want you to understand me, because I know my body, and I'm paying the bills. I will rise to meet this challenge. I will walk–and walk well. I'm going to be home by May 1–no wheelchair, no crutches, no cane."

"But, Mr. Brinker," protested the physicians, "you're not a doctor. And we're telling you that you're sick."

"Yeah, I know I'm sick," he replied. "But I'm going to get well quicker than you think."

The Brinkers then set out to build a team dedicated to helping Norman get back to normal. "That's the same spirit we have at Brinker International," said Norman. "If something comes up, you get your team together."

They already had the doctors, nurses, and nutritionists. And the three areas in which they needed help included physical and occupational therapy and speech-language pathology. So two physical therapists were chosen to help Norm regain general motor skills, which include moving, balancing, sitting, standing, and walking.

This was the one area where he needed the most help. After having been in a coma for two and one-half weeks, Norman was weak and tired. He had to rebuild his strength and coordination. And, as he had no feeling on his left side, exercise, massaging, and sensory input were critical treatments.

One occupational therapist was chosen to help hone fine motor skills and activities of daily living (commonly referred to as ADLs). For instance, Norman had to learn how to shave, eat, and dress with a paralyzed left arm.

In addition to his left arm and leg being paralyzed, so were the muscles on the left side of his face and mouth–which, of course, affected his ability both to swallow and to speak. As a result, a speech-language pathologist was selected to help Norman with his motor speech patterns. Fortunately, his cognitive skills were not severely affected. The head injury caused some temporary impairment of his ability to recall, organize, and synthesize information. But, interestingly enough, Norman suffered absolutely no impairment of his language skills. He was able to utilize his memory to produce language that was grammatically correct, rational, and coherent.

The serious nature of Norman's head injury had also resulted in a condition known as dysarthria–an impairment where the patient knows in his head what he wants to say, but has difficulty articulating and resonating the message. This was to be a short-lived occurrence that was eventually worked out with therapy. His speech-language pathologist was assigned to help work all these skills and abilities back into a normal condition.

Once the entire team was selected, Norman and Nancy got them all together and set clear, concrete goals—with intermediate steps to achieve those goals. "We then obtained a calendar and talked to the therapists," recalled Norman. "We backtracked from May 1 and set our goals. We were going to have me standing by this date, walking by that date, and so on."

Norman also set an interim goal of April 22 to fly back to Dallas to receive in person a Business Statesman Award—which was being given to him by the Harvard Business School Alumni Club. In addition, he set three general priorities for himself while at Pinecrest: First and foremost, he was going to work on his physical rehabilitation. Second, he wanted to be familiarized and conversant with the numerical aspects of his business. And third, he would exercise his memory and reestablish personal relationships.

With his goals set, and his team in place, it was time to take action. But Norman's performance was driven by several ethereal elements of his character. They are common threads that propel people into action—that help leaders to achieve.

For instance, Norman's high rate of energy, physical fitness, and competitive nature contributed to his eventual recovery. He had taken care of himself all his life and truly believed that while he was in the coma, his body had gone into second gear to take care of him. "I was not afraid," he would later say. "From experiencing all those other accidents, I learned to listen to Mother Nature and work at my recoveries."

Moreover, he is the kind of person who would never give up. It wasn't enough for him just to survive; he wanted to be 100 percent recovered. Norman's perseverance, optimism, and self-confidence made a significant difference in physical rehabilitation—and on the attitude of the members of his team.

"Mentally," he said, "I've always been attuned to solving the problem, whether it was physical or something else. When I had a problem, my father said: 'Little Boy, you have to learn to take care of yourself. You got into it, you get out of it.' Well, I got into this situation by myself, so, as far as I was concerned, it was just another challenge to get out of it."

And there was one more less tangible component that spurred Norman Brinker into his determined, almost obsessive drive to a meaningful recovery: the kind and caring support of so many people who were pulling for him.

By now, Norman had received thousands of cards, letters, faxes, and phone calls. "If these people had such a wonderful concern about me, then I was sure going to respond," he recalled. "So when I had a tendency to be down and dour, I'd just take some of those cards and read them—and that picked me up right away."

"I've got to show them I appreciate their support," he told himself at the time. "I've got to make it back."

∾

AT PINECREST, Norman established small goals for himself and then set out to achieve them. First he worked on his left arm until he began to sense some feeling. Finally, it moved a little. "My left arm came back rather quickly," he recalled. "After that, I started to work on my left leg. I was positive I could make it function if I was determined enough."

But Norman's leg took longer to come around. Eventually, though, he began to feel his ankle. "I just know that sensation will move up to my knee, and I will walk well again," he told Nancy confidently.

In all, it took about three weeks for the paralysis on the left side of Norman's body to begin to dissipate by small increments. Then the real work began—the labor involved in training his body to become totally functional again.

Norman's routine at Pinecrest was busy and tiring. Nearly every minute of his day, six days a week, was taken up with physical therapy, occupational therapy, and speech-language pathology—not to mention regular exercise that included stretching and light weight lifting.

His physical therapists, Robyn Stephens Budine and Erin Fay Azzato, worked with their patient a minimum of four hours each day. "They were bright, positive, and well-organized," recalled Norm. "And they were absolutely insistent on doing things correctly and making everything work well."

Norman's personal rule during his daily grind was "steady progress coupled with courteousness and optimism."

It all began with the simplest of tasks: Sitting up on the side of the bed for eight minutes, then lying down, then sitting up for eight minutes again. After he could do that drill regularly, it was time to stand—something Norman had not done since the polo accident on January 21.

As he sat on the edge of his bed, Robyn and Erin placed a hospital side table in front of him for support. They stood next to him and slowly, steadily, helped him to his feet. Norm held his balance, and the women let go ever so gently. As the tips of their fingers left his arms, they backed away a few feet.

It was March 5, 1993, and though a bit wobbly, Norman Brinker smiled. "Okay," he said. "I'm standing up. It's a wonderful day."

For the first few exercises involving standing, Norman rose, counted to ten, and sat down. Next he stood for ten minutes at a time, leaning on the table, shifting his weight from left to right. Then he sat down again.

Shortly thereafter, a set routine was repeated in earnest, over and over and over again: Sit down. Lie on your back. Roll over on your side. Sit up. Touch your nose. Reach up. Reach back. Shake hands with your left hand. Bring your hand up over your head and, with a controlled movement, bring it back down. Stand up. Shift your weight. Sit down. Lie on your back. Roll over on your side. Sit up.

The routine rarely varied. And when Norman had mastered it fully, his team's attention turned to walking–and walking without assistance. But that proved as difficult as anything he had ever attempted. Essentially, he had to learn how to walk all over again.

The team broke down the components of walking, which included such things as muscle coordination and balance. Stretching to limber up; twisting around and catching balls to sharpen eye-hand skills; tiny steps; one at first, then five at a time, then sit down and rest.

The two therapists would move Norman's left leg forward as he tried to walk, and the right leg followed naturally. He began by taking one step, then two steps, then five steps at a time. Quickly, Norman worked up to ten steps, leaning on the wheeled table as it moved forward, slowly away from the bed; then it was ten steps backward to the bed.

After he had mastered this early drill on walking, Erin asked Norman how he felt. "Well," he responded, "I'm tired but not exhausted. But just think of it, four weeks ago, I was in a coma. Ten days ago, I couldn't move my left arm. And five days ago, I couldn't sit up by myself. I'm really looking forward to the next five days."

Norman's progress began to increase in speed and duration. The therapists got rid of the table, and he now walked by leaning on their shoulders. Actually, it was something like a dance routine, with either Erin or Robyn issuing their patient commands. "Okay, Norman, tighten those hips. Move that left foot forward. We're building your muscles back up to strength. A little bigger steps, now. Shift your weight. Okay, let's turn around and go back."

Before and after his physical therapy sessions, Norman spent two hours each day with an occupational therapist honing his skills in activities of daily living. There, he practiced such simple tasks as standing up while holding a glass of water–first in the right hand, then in the left hand, then with both hands.

He worked on writing, on shaving, and on dressing himself. "I had brushed my own teeth and combed my hair from the beginning," Norman recalled. "But the first time I put on my pants, it took me ten minutes. I couldn't lift my left leg high enough."

The therapist also had Norman work on his balance by taking his shirt off while standing up, dropping it on the floor, picking it up, and then putting it back on again–and tucking it in. "I really struggled to accomplish simple tasks that all of us take for granted," he remembered.

And just when Norman thought he was really doing great, his therapist informed him one evening that he was going to have to tie his own shoes the next day. "That concerned me, because I still didn't have much dexterity in the fingers of my left hand," he said. "So that night I put the shoes on my bed and practiced tying and untying them for two hours. I wanted to be ready the next morning."

He surprised everybody when he sat on the side of the bed, put his shoes on, and then leaned over to tie them both while his feet were stationary on the floor. "It took me a few minutes to put on that left one," remembered Norman," but I tied those shoes."

And then one day, recalled Norman, "They took me outside, and Robyn let go of my hand. 'You're on your own,' she said. 'You have to walk down the sidewalk to Erin.'

"She must have been fifty yards away," said Norm, "or at least that's what it looked like to me at the time. I had to stop every four or five steps to rest. It was grueling both mentally and physically—but twenty minutes later I was there. I did it."

Three weeks later, Norman set a goal of walking to the Wal-Mart store about a quarter of a mile away. "I thought I had bitten off more than I could chew on that one," he remembered. "But when I made it I was so proud of myself—and so completely exhausted that I just wanted to stop and rest. Then Robyn said: 'Okay, Norman. You're halfway done. Now let's walk back.'"

~

AS NORMAN'S RECOVERY STEADILY PROGRESSED, he received more and more visitors. In addition to family, close friends like Max Fisher, Ross Perot, Ira Harris, and Dick Heath came by to encourage and cheer him on.

Perot stopped in at a Florida Chili's for lunch just before he visited his friend at Pinecrest. "The employees there came up to me and inquired about Norman's health," said Perot. "But that wasn't an unusual thing. Policemen would often ask me: 'How's Mr. Brinker?' And when I appeared on *CBS This Morning*, Paula Zahn asked me how Norman was before we went on the air."

Ross was particularly moved by the people in Chili's organization, most of whom had tears in their eyes when they talked about Norman. "That type of emotion cannot be generated from a distance," he said. "Brinker had met most of those people personally. He goes to many openings of restaurants and visits them whenever possible. Not only that, Norman goes into the kitchen to see the chefs to pat them on the back and ask how they're doing. He builds personal bonds with nearly everybody he meets."

Keeping his personal and business relationships going was always on Norman's mind. In fact, he made it an overall part of the rehabilitation process while at Pinecrest.

Norm would take time in between his structured activities to work on his business acumen, to hone skills, to review company spreadsheets and other documents—and to refamiliarize himself with the people he worked with on a regular basis.

On one visit, Dr. Sandy Carden recalled seeing Norman in bed with all his corporate papers scattered around. "He had pictures of all the directors on Brinker International's board, all the top administrators, and all the corporate leadership," recalled Dr. Carden. "He was practicing. He was memorizing and recognizing the faces of people he knew perfectly well before his injury—but he had to re-remember them."

Dr. Carden was simply amazed. "Actually, Norman could recognize people and come up with their names on the spot better than most people *after* his accident. He disciplined himself so strenuously, he was able to recover well beyond what the doctors thought was possible—and much faster than a person with average motivation. He was absolutely determined to get back to his company as fast as possible."

Carden was certainly correct in that statement. By the first of April, Norm began to call many of the executives at Brinker International. When he realized that there was no way to reach everybody personally, he sent a telephone voice-mail message to employees around the country, thanking them for their cards and prayers and, in turn, expressing his own affection for them. In that message,

Norman also vowed he'd be back at work in early May.

By the first of April, after meeting with the directors and therapists at Pinecrest, doctors allowed Norman to return to his home in Palm Beach and attend the rehabilitation center on an outpatient basis. For the next full month, he came back religiously to work with his therapists to gain as much strength and endurance as possible.

He repeated walking exercises up and down the halls of the center. He practiced walking with a cane—but quickly threw it away. He walked up and down the building's outside steps, hit some golf balls, and he tried to jog for the first time. He also worked on his balance by carrying a full briefcase—just as he would do if he were at work.

As April 22 approached, Norman felt confident that he could travel to Dallas to receive the Business Statesman Award. Several close friends, however, advised him to stay with the therapy and send a video of his acceptance remarks instead—which he did. "I felt so elated about how the therapy was going," Norman remembered, "I thought it was best to stay another ten days or so to get ready for the May 4 board meeting." Norman remained flexible enough to skip an interim goal—but dedicated enough to stick with his overriding mission, which was to be at that meeting.

The better he got, the more bored he became. He had already refamiliarized himself with his business. He was walking and talking very well. What would occupy his remaining time at Pinecrest? Well, much to the chagrin of the rehabilitation center, Norman began to evaluate the center itself.

They had too many people doing the same thing, he determined. He told the management there how they could more efficiently staff the hospital floor—and how they could run the stations, the physical therapy units, and the cafeteria so that fewer people could work in them and more could get done. However, his real objective at the center was to encourage and support many other patients who were not doing as well.

"That's when I knew he had not suffered any permanent injuries to his analytical skills and abilities," said Nancy. "That's when we all knew that any possible long-term disabilities he might suffer would be motor-related and more physical in nature."

Shortly before his planned return to Dallas, Norman had dinner at Grady's American Grill, a Brinker International restaurant. Employees were astounded when they saw him walk in by himself and quickly gathered around to greet him. Before and after eating, he mixed with nearly everybody in the restaurant. He went back to the kitchen and talked to the cooks and dishwashers. And he moved from table to table, cordially asking customers their opinions of the restaurant and how the food tasted.

"I felt like I witnessed a miracle," said Pete Schenkel, a friend who had dined with him. "He was the same Norman Brinker I knew before the accident."

~

JUST BEFORE LEAVING PINECREST, Norman was given a rousing send-off by Robyn and Erin, the two women who had guided him through physical therapy; who had spent the most time with him.

"I can't thank you enough," he told them. "This was a potentially very tragic situation. And here I am feeling good about it. It would not be this way if it hadn't been for you. Six weeks ago, I couldn't even stand up without help. You helped me—and made me valuable and worthwhile. I will always be thankful and grateful for your help and determination."

These were the women who had never seen their patient depressed, angry, or complaining in any way. To them, he had always been courteous, sincere, and good-natured. "And you know what," said one of the women. "You've really done a lot for us, too–in teaching us more about people and about the importance of positive thinking and goal-setting. We appreciate that. Thank you, Norman. God bless you."

10.

"Norman walked in with an empty briefcase. He respected the culture that was already there and then tried to enhance it with his own. It was like putting gasoline with fire–it just really took off!"

CREED FORD, VICE PRESIDENT,
explaining Norman's entrance into the Chili's organization

"I don't send for people. For the most part I go to other people's offices to see them instead of having them come to me. It's part of my culture."

NORMAN BRINKER,
when asked how often he summoned people up to his office

"In this company, we really care about each other."

NORMAN BRINKER,
1995

Chili's and Brinker International

On Sunday morning, July 3, 1983, after a restless first night at Presbyterian Hospital, Norman telephoned Larry Lavine. "Larry," he said, "I'm sorry I won't be able to come in on Tuesday. I had a polo accident yesterday, and I've got some fractured ribs and a paralyzed liver and spleen. Oh, and my back hurts, too."

"Norman, that's terrible," responded Lavine, who then jokingly quipped, "Well, maybe we'll just come to you and have the meeting right there in the hospital room."

"That's right!" Norman replied enthusiastically. "That's exactly what we're going to do. We'll have the meeting on Tuesday morning. Let's have everybody here by nine."

"Norman," protested Larry, "I was just kidding."

"No, really," said Norman. "It's already set up. See you then."

When the staff doctor came by on his morning rounds sometime later, Norm informed him of the meeting he was going to hold and asked that some extra chairs be sent up to his room. "Absolutely not! No way!" said the physician. "You cannot have a meeting in here. You're in no condition to be seeing anybody—much less conducting business."

The doctor then placed a sign on the outside of Norman's door that read: NO VISITORS ALLOWED.

But the first thing Tuesday morning, Norman called Ducky Bob's, a party supply company, and ordered a dozen chairs. "I'm in room 612, and don't let anybody stop you," he said.

As the deliverymen were walking through the lobby and heading toward the elevators, a hospital receptionist tried to hold them back: "Hey, wait a minute. Where are you going with those?" she asked. "Brinker's room," was the terse reply. And when they got to the sixth floor, they were puzzled by the No Visitors sign but delivered the chairs as instructed.

The next call Norman made was to Creed Ford, vice president of operations at Chili's main office. "Hi, Creed, what's going on?"

"Well, we're just starting our operations meeting," said Creed.

"Didn't Larry mention coming over here to the hospital?" asked Norman.

"Yeah, but we all thought you were kidding."

"Oh, no. Please come on over and bring everybody with you. I'm ready to go."

"When I hung up the phone," recalled Creed, "I informed everyone we were going to have our meeting at the hospital a couple of blocks away. And our reactions were all similar: 'What the hell is this all about?' we thought."

Few of Chili's executive managers had actually even met Norman Brinker—and many were skeptical of him. After all, he had been one of their chief competitors, their enemy. They wondered what was he going to be like. Was he going to be a dictator who barked out orders? Was he going to instill the Steak & Ale culture into their organization? Was he going to clean house? In general, they took a cautious, wait-and-see attitude into that first meeting.

At approximately 9:30 A.M., a dozen executives paraded into Norman's hospital room. When he saw them, he grabbed the lift bar hanging from the ceiling and slowly pulled himself up. "Hi, everybody," he said with a smile. "I didn't intend to be in this condition for our first meeting, and I apologize if I've inconvenienced anybody."

Everyone then took a seat around the bed, with Creed Ford sitting in the center and Larry Lavine off to the side. The meeting began with Norman stating how excited he was to be a part of their team. "We could see that he was in a great deal of pain, but hiding it well," recalled Larry.

Creed asked for a few key reports on the prior week's earnings. As the numbers were given, Norman made some encouraging comments to reinforce the positive results.

Then he interrupted the usual routine of the meeting. "Say," he said, "let's discuss what Chili's is all about. What is Chili's? Who are we, anyway? Creed, get your flip chart out. You can be the scribe."

Right away a few eyes rolled, and some arms folded. "This is ridiculous," thought Creed.

"Well, what are we?" inquired Norman.

"Well," said one individual. "We're profitable, and we're fun."

"Okay," said Norman, "write those down. Everything's fair game. There are no bad answers."

"We're quality," said another. And the list went on until Creed had filled up four pages of the flip chart.

"Okay," Norman said at that point. "Now, let's critique each of these things."

"Let's talk about profitability. We're profitable in comparison to what?" he asked. "What is our average unit sales?"

"Well," came the reply, "we're doing about $ 1.5 million per unit."

"Okay, what's Bennigan's doing?"

"Well, they're over $ 2.4 million."

"What's your bottom line been lately?"

"It's been roughly six percent PBT [Profit Before Tax]."

"Okay, what should it be?"

"Well, hopefully, it really should be ten percent."

"Okay," asked Norman. "Are we really profitable or not?"

"Well," replied a member of the team, "we're probably not as profitable as we should be—or need to be if we are to really grow."

The conversation then turned to quality. "Are we quality?" they asked themselves. "What about the soft tacos? Are *they* quality?"

"Well, not really. They could be better," came the consensus.

"Okay," said Norman, "we've defined a couple of opportunities for us to concentrate on."

As the meeting continued, arms unfolded, and people became more and more engaged. They paced around the room and became active participants.

After about two hours, the group took a break, and Nancy and her mother, Ellie, came in with prepared dishes of baked beans, brownies, and King Ranch Chicken. "Pretty tasty, huh?" said Norman. "What do you think? Are these something we might add to the menu eventually?"

After it was over, everybody felt more comfortable with Norman as a member of the team. "Right from the very first meeting, he earned respect from all of us," recalled Creed. The executives were also impressed with the drill Norman had introduced them to. "Asking who we were, critiquing those things, and then developing new opportunities—really made a lot of sense after we'd experienced the technique," said Creed. "It was apparent that he really had a lot to bring to the table."

Norman's experience with capital markets also played a big role in this early planning phase of Chili's development. Both he and Larry Lavine recognized that, with $8 million worth of debt and a $7 million credit line, they clearly did not have the financial ability either to expand or be competitive. So a goal was set to go public sometime around the middle of December 1983.

Because of past relationships, the addition of his presence at Chili's was a positive for the public offering, and Norman's prior investment banking relationships helped assure a good price for the stock. "I picked up the phone and called Dan Cook at Goldman Sachs," recalled Norman, "and asked him if he'd help Chili's go public just like he helped Steak & Ale. I let him know it was important to get going right away."

When Norman finally recovered enough to come to the office (which was about a week after the first meeting), he went out into the field and conducted the "who are we?" drills with everyone in the company—including food servers and local managers. Within a month, Norman visited all twenty-five Chili's restaurants in Dallas, San Antonio, California, Colorado, Kansas, Georgia, and Florida. And, within three months, he had personally met every employee at Chili's *and* heard their ideas about current operations and what they wanted to see done in the future.

Back at headquarters in Dallas, Norm worked long hours in an effort to understand Chili's corporate culture, its operations, and its existing financial structure. One evening about eight, Creed Ford was in his office working when he saw Norman walk by rather rapidly—and then back in the opposite direction just as fast. About ten minutes later, he came back and stuck his head in: "I haven't figured out how this whole thing works," said Norman with a bewildered look on his face. "But I'm going to figure it out." And then he turned around and walked off before Creed had a chance to say anything.

"I remember Norman working very diligently at trying to gain a clear understanding of what we did well, and what we needed to do to move forward," Creed recalled. "He did not come in with a set agenda. Whereas some people would have come in with a briefcase full of plans and slides, Norman walked in with an empty briefcase and said: 'Okay, before I recommend anything, I'm going to find out about the organization as it exists today.' He respected the culture that was already there and then tried to enhance it with his own ideas."

Before Brinker, Chili's expertise was clearly in taking care of the customer, taking care of the service, and taking care of the quality of food. While that focus would never be compromised, all the executives eventually agreed with Norman that if they were to have a significant expansion in the number of Chili's restaurants, they would need to broaden their expertise in the areas of marketing, strategic planning, and finance, and expand the menu for a broader base of customers.

The company then set out to attract the most talented people it could find to fill the gaps in its team. "We let the word get out to the people in the marketplace," said Norman. "We also used personal contacts, and ran some advertisements in restaurant magazines and newspapers around the country."

Over a period of time, several key industry people came over to Chili's, if for no other reason than to be associated with Norman Brinker. Ron McDougall would head up Chili's strategic development effort, Eddie Palms would work on prototypes for the company's new buildings, John Titus would develop real estate, and Hal Smith, former chairman and CEO of S & A, came over to be president. And after a short period of time, even Marvin Braddock (who had been with Norman at San Diego State, Jack-In-The-Box, and Steak & Ale) joined the Chili's team to contribute his expertise in purchasing.

Norman wanted the best people for the jobs, because he knew that he could not possibly do everything himself—and because he believed a team is so much stronger than any individual. "Why not get the best and the smartest," he would say. "After all, sinners can repent, but stupidity is forever."

Norman chose McDougall, Palms, Titus, and others not only because they were talented in their own right, but also because they worked well in a team environment. "I was not interested at all in people who wanted to be individual stars," said Norman. "I never have been."

Once the team was assembled, they collectively and immediately began looking to the future. "We had a six-month window before we went public to generate the capital we needed to fuel the system," recalled Norman. "And we strategically used that time period to put together our comprehensive plan of action."

That plan included everything from a strategic marketing effort (led by McDougall), to determine specific geographic and industry markets—all the way to the variety of food on the menu. And it included this mission statement, which was generated by the executive team with input from employees in the field:

> *We aim to be a premier growth company with a balanced approach toward people, quality, and profits; to cultivate customer loyalty by listening to, caring about and providing customers with a quality dining experience; to enhance a high level of ethics, excellence, innovation and integrity; to attract, develop and retain a superior team; to be focused, sensitive and responsive to our employees and their environment, and to enhance long-term shareholder growth.*

In order to craft their plan, the team started gathering information and performing detailed research. They sent out a message to all Chili's people that ideas were wanted. Everyone, from the dishwasher to the accountant to the chairman, was encouraged to make suggestions to improve the game plan. "Our goal," said Norman Brinker, "is to create and perpetuate the building of something of lasting value."

159

Good ideas to that end were rewarded with bonuses, eventual stock options, and/or salary increases. "While we don't care who gets the credit because we want the team to win," Norman explained, "we also feel it's critical to reward individual performance. That's why we pay our people well and have extra incentives. There's no doubt about it—compensation can be a great motivator when leveraged properly."

They began to study the desires of customers, demographics, and the restaurant industry in general. Much of their data came directly from patrons in restaurants. But rather than conducting surveys with a clipboard and questionnaire, the group simply went out to the restaurants and listened to people.

On one visit to the field, a group of middle-aged couples enthusiastically told Norman that they frequented Chili's when their children came home from college. "The kids really love it," they said.

"They really meant it as a compliment," said Norm, "but I took it as a death knell, because they were saying that primarily this restaurant appealed to young people. As a matter of fact, I heard the same thing from many other customers as well."

Norman then asked his team whether they needed to act to correct the perception that Chili's was only for young people. After all, at the time, more than 60 percent of sales were from gourmet burgers that were eight ounces, cooked-to-order, and served in a basket. The restaurants were high-quality, informal, and a lot of fun. But the team agreed that a change had to be made if they were to expand beyond the youth market. Accordingly, they set a goal to expand their customer base to include people twenty-five to fifty years old.

Frequent excursions were also made to other establishments to sample the food and view customer reactions. For example, on one trip to an On The Border restaurant,

Norman was particularly impressed with the fajita dinner. One of the managers said that Chili's had talked about fajitas earlier, but abandoned the idea because they didn't have the capital to remodel all the kitchens and put in charcoal broilers, flat-top grills, and beefed-up hood systems to handle smoke. "Well," he replied, "we'll have the capital in January. Why don't we set a goal to put fajitas on the menu. We can do this," he said, pointing at what On The Border had already started.

After collecting all the data, Chili's comprehensive plan included a vastly expanded menu of chicken fajitas, salads, grilled sandwiches, steaks, and barbecue ribs. Furthermore, a meal was to cost less than eight dollars per person, with drinks.

"We also evaluated a lot of little things that many other restaurant chains normally overlook," said Norman. For example, in redesigning their prototype buildings, Chili's engineers calculated the average number of steps that each waiter took to get from the kitchen to a table. From that data, the restaurant was configured to decrease the average number of steps by forty. "Little things like that should give us a decided competitive edge in the long run."

Their plans also included the touch and feel of the restaurants. "Ambience is a vital part of the dining experience," said Norman. "We had to make certain that our guests would feel comfortable when they came in and sat down."

The team planned to replace the hamburger baskets with china, to add more side items to the menu, and they even discussed how the servers should approach customers. When someone asked Norman if he wanted them to say: "Hi, I'm Mike, I'll be your waiter tonight," just like they used to at Steak & Ale, Norman's response was: "No, I don't think so. That's been overdone. Just ask them to go up and say whatever they think is friendly and right."

By the end of December 1983, members of the Chili's management team had completed their comprehensive plan and were just itching to start making changes. Moreover, they were excited to begin with their number-one priority, which was to have an orderly expansion in the number of Chili's restaurants. When they went public on January 6, 1984, millions of dollars were infused into the company–and the team set off to implement the plan aggressively.

∽

A WEEK OR SO AFTER her husband's company first appeared in the New York Stock Exchange listings–on a cold January evening close to midnight–Nancy Brinker discovered a lump on her breast. Previously, she'd had three benign lumps removed, but this one felt different–not large and rubbery like the others, but smaller and harder. It grew noticeably over a period of days, and a subsequent biopsy revealed cancer.

Nancy was frightened, confused, angry, and tearful. But the doctors reassured her. The lump was small, they said, and it had been detected very early. There was every reason to believe she would have a complete and swift recovery. Norman and Ellie rushed to Nancy's side–and both assured her that they were certain she'd be all right.

After thinking over the options carefully, Nancy opted for a mastectomy that was performed the morning after the positive diagnosis. After recovering from the surgical procedure, she underwent four courses of chemotherapy that, subsequently, resulted in several serious side effects–including complete hair loss.

It was a tough time for Norman–not as tough as for Nancy, but tough, nonetheless. In front of his wife, he was all positive. In private moments, however, he was distressed and anxious. Fifteen years before, he had watched helplessly as Maureen died. Her death had been a harsh lesson in the reality and fragility of life. Again, he felt helpless. All he could do was reassure her, love her, and see that she received the best medical care possible.

On Nancy's first evening back home, Norman held her tight and convinced her that he loved her exactly the same as he had before her operation. He stayed with her through the chemotherapy, the loss of her hair, and eventual reconstructive surgery. "Norman tried to keep me smiling throughout," recalled Nancy. "And he did a good job of it."

Nancy Brinker eventually made a complete recovery. Moreover, she went on to create, build, and organize the Susan G. Komen Foundation into the largest and most successful breast-cancer organization in the world. Her experience in personally handling the medical details of her own nightmare, combined with already well-honed leadership skills, gave her a new insight and a new passion in helping other women face the disease with hope and courage.

~

NANCY'S CANCER HAD OCCURRED at the very moment when Chili's was just getting off the ground—just as Maureen's had occurred when Steak & Ale was beginning to grow. But, as she began feeling better, Nancy encouraged Norman to stay involved in his new business enterprise. And with that kind of optimism and reassurance, Norman got moving.

When Chili's went public, Brinker and his team upgraded all existing facilities, remodeled every kitchen, revamped the menus and service routine, and began building more restaurants. Essentially, the entire Chili's organization enacted change in an extraordinarily rapid manner—with enthusiasm and determination. "It's a funny thing about change," Norman once said. "Everybody's afraid of it when they don't know how it's going to affect them. But when they are part of it, the fear goes away. That's one reason, throughout

my career, I've tried to involve everybody and listen carefully to their ideas."

As Chili's began to change and grow, Norman strategically created tremendous attention to the concept of
gourmet burgers—which were still a major fixture on the
menu. In many minds, the simple fact that he left Pillsbury
to go with Chili's validated the gourmet burger segment of
the casual dining industry.

Almost instantly, look-alike restaurants began springing
up around the country in attempts to emulate the Chili's
plan. As a result, competition for that particular segment of
the consumer market intensified beyond all expectations.

As soon as they sensed the increased activity, the team
assembled. "Look," said Norman, "we can only grow so fast
on our own. If we're going to win this battle, there's no way
that we can internally build the number of units we'll need to
compete. Why don't we concentrate on the areas it's easy for
us to get into, and where we'll make the most money? The
areas that we don't think we'll get to within the next three to
five years, we can either joint-venture or franchise out."

Creed Ford recalled the team's initial reaction to
Norman's suggestion: "Our first response was not to do
that," he said. "We wanted to do it all ourselves so we could
keep control. But Norman worked to persuade us he was
right, and the group eventually realized that there was no
other way to outflank the competition. It just takes too long
to get into a new area and get to know that market. Some
local guy would surely beat us to the punch."

Essentially, Norman convinced the Chili's management
team that they had a better chance of success if they let local
people—with knowledge of the market, real estate ownership, and restaurant experience—expand their business in
areas that Chili's could not afford to enter immediately.

Once they were convinced it was the right thing to do,
the team aggressively set out to recruit joint venture and

franchise partners around the country. The first place they concentrated on was Florida, where they only had one restaurant. Norman called up his longtime friend Gene Knippers, who had worked with him to set up Steak & Ale restaurants there years ago. Knippers took on a fifty-fifty deal for Florida, Georgia, and Alabama. Four years later, after a number of restaurants were constructed and profitable, Chili's bought out Knippers' interest.

Such an innovative plan for expansion proved to be faster, better, and safer than if Chili's had tried to do everything on its own. Effectively, the group had halved its investment risk on the chances of failure.

Once the competition got wind of what Norman was doing, interesting things began to happen. For example, one executive working for a competitor called Chili's and offered two or three prime sites in exchange for a joint venture in Northern California and Nevada. A deal was cut, and five years later, after the opening of several successful restaurants, his interest was also purchased.

And so it went. There was a major franchise arrangement worked out with the Chesapeake Bay Company in Virginia, with Dunkin' Donuts in Connecticut and the Boston area, and with several smaller companies throughout Pennsylvania.

Chili's quickly spread across the country by leveraging its assets on a state-by-state basis. The company expanded nationally with three overall strategies:

1. One hundred percent Chili's owned and operated.
2. Fifty percent interest with joint-venture partners.
3. Franchise operations.

However, because of the high risk of international operations—which Norman had experienced with Burger King—no capital investment of any kind was made outside the United States. So the company not only leveraged a local partner, it also leveraged that partner's financial assets. All international Chili's outlets were franchised with a royalty on gross sales. Each franchisee paid a fee, depending on how expansive the area was and how many stores were built. Chili's, of course, did make a substantial monetary and philosophical investment in training and indoctrination to operations and culture.

The Chili's team constantly planned for the future. In July of each year, it knew exactly how many restaurants it was going to open during the following calendar year. Such planning was part of Norman's bias toward constant and planned achievement.

From his first days at Jack-In-The-Box, he concentrated on long-term growth. "I've always been in a growing mode," he'd say. "We've got to look at the big picture over a substantial period of time. We're either going to win in the long run—or lose in the short term."

～

ONCE CHILI'S INITIAL EXPANSION TOOK EFFECT, total sales went up dramatically, and bottom-line profits increased accordingly. As a result, the next several years were filled with substantial stock price gains that pleased everybody—employees and stockholders alike.

But as the early growth process began to hum along, Norman started thinking of the future. He remembered what happened at Steak & Ale when they had to conceive Bennigan's in order to continue to grow at a rapid pace. "What about new concepts and new restaurants for Chili's?" he asked his team. "Just because we're only one restaurant concept now doesn't mean we should stay that way."

In mid-1984, Norman attended the Multi-Unit Food Services Operators (MUFSO) Convention in Washington, D.C., where he heard that a small chain of restaurants in Tennessee named Grady's was planning to go public. Norman was familiar with Grady's from visits to Knoxville and knew the firm was very high volume, with specialties in prime rib, steaks, and baby-back ribs. Within a couple of months, Chili's owned Grady's.

Not long after that acquisition, while out in the field checking on Chili's competition, Norman decided to stop in at Fuddrucker's—a successful gourmet hamburger chain in San Antonio. He was so impressed with the quality of the food and the ambience of the restaurant that, before leaving, he gave the cashier his card and asked that the owner, Phil Romano, call him. "Well, I'll tell him," she said, "but he never returns phone calls, so I don't know what will happen."

It wasn't until October of 1989, five years later, that Romano called Brinker. "Hi, Norman," he said. "I'm Phil Romano and I'm returning your call. I didn't want to call until I had something of real interest to show you."

What Romano had to show him was a new restaurant called Macaroni Grill that he had built and was successfully testing (also in the San Antonio area). Norman listened to Phil's idea with interest and then asked Lane Cardwell, vice president of strategic planning, to go down to check it out. Within two weeks, Lane, having made a site visit, returned with a glowing report, and the entire Chili's management team, Norman included, dined at Romano's Macaroni Grill.

What they found was an innovative concept patterned after restaurants in Italy. It had an "open-market" ambience to it—with choice meats, fresh vegetables, and a variety of pasta in temperature-controlled glass cases near the entrance.

Chefs prepared meals in a kitchen in full view of customers, who could not only see chickens roasting in brick ovens, but also could smell the appetite-whetting aromas. Romano placed a gallon jug of wine on each table from which patrons served themselves. At the end of the meal, in an honor system of sorts, customers told servers how many glasses of wine they had consumed.

Moreover, waiters, waitresses, and hosts were all young and vibrant–just as Brinker liked it. Romano's idea fit right in with the Chili's concept–so the team scooped up the Macaroni Grill for $4.5 million in newly issued Chili's stock.

Norman liked the idea of buying an established restaurant concept that already had some time under its belt. "It's a very expensive and long process to start something from scratch," he said. "There's also a high rate of risk involved, because it'll take about three years before you really know whether or not a new concept is going to succeed."

But that risk did not stop Norman Brinker from encouraging Chili's executives to develop new restaurant ideas in-house. As a matter of fact, when he made it known that he would like to start doing so, employees flooded his office with exciting ideas.

In effect, Chili's set up a process that turned out to be something of a "research and development" (R&D) technique to test the market's reaction to new ideas. The company opened the Border Stop Steak House in Houston in a converted Chili's unit. "It was a kind of live R&D," said Norman, "where products were tested to see if people liked it or not." In this particular case, the concept didn't work out, so Norman had it closed down.

"You've got to take risks in business," said Norman. "If a person came up with a unique idea, I thought it was best to let them run with it. Who knows, eventually one might work. One great success can pay for a hundred failures–if you don't let your ego take control."

Even though the chains were operated as separate entities, they also worked in tandem to maximize profits–especially when it came to restaurant locations. For example, Norman had seen over the years that when competing restaurants opened on the same block, rather than business being hurt, it often boomed. So the company began to look for potential locations that would house multiple restaurants. The idea was to control an intersection and put a different concept on each corner. "People like restaurant rows," he explained. "If you've got a group, and somebody decides they don't want Italian, they can cross the street and eat Mexican."

Eventually, it became a common sight around the country to see Chili's, Macaroni Grill, Grady's, and Cozymel's (or some combination) at a busy intersection in a major metropolitan area.

~

ONCE NEW RESTAURANT CHAINS WERE CONCEIVED, constructed, nurtured, and finally deemed successful– Norman encouraged a process of continual renewal and reevaluation. He believed everything has a life cycle that generally runs in seven-year increments. "Every seven years, we really need to be making some major changes before the original concept gets tired," he constantly advocated. "Upgrading and evolution, however, must be ongoing.

"Increased competition necessitates constant tinkering, constant change," said Norman to the people at Chili's. "We must stay at least a half step ahead of the competition. We should always be asking ourselves: 'What can we do better, quicker and with more imagination?'"

In order to answer that question, Norman persistently monitored customer needs, lifestyle changes, and patterns of dining activity. For example, in the early 1990s, he noticed that the amount of spices sold in the United States was up five or six times since 1970 because of a gradually changing palate. That change also coincided with a trend to make healthier foods more tasty. "No matter how healthy a food is," said Norman, "if it doesn't taste good, it won't work."

To meet the demand, Chili's increased the use of spices, added more salads, and smaller portions to the menu. "We also went from animal fats to vegetable oil for preparation of fried foods. Vegetable oil is low in fat," said Norman, "but it's also more expensive. And when you make that kind of change in hundreds of restaurants, the costs really add up. But that's what it takes to win customers of the baby boomer generation."

Norman also noticed a major lifestyle change from the 1970s to the 1990s that went from the "devil-may-care," "let-it-all-hang-out" attitude of many young, single people–to a conservative, monogamous, and discriminating palate of older, more settled married couples. "People started driving around in minivans and pickup trucks as opposed to sports cars and sedans," recalled Norman. "To us, that indicated there was going to be more takeout, more eating on the run, and more families in the restaurants."

Additionally, because more than 50 percent of married women were working and, therefore, not seeing their children all day, kids became more and more a part of eating out. So Norman made certain that parents knew that children were welcome at all his restaurants. "In the 1970s, we opened with only two high chairs," he said. "In the nineties we didn't dare begin without at least a dozen on hand."

∽

EVERY YEAR, without fail, Norman journeyed to Florida to participate in the Palm Beach Polo and Country Club's Challenge Cup tournament. It seemed as if he had a serious polo accident every four or five years, and, sure enough, during a February 1989 match, he collided with another horse and was catapulted out of the saddle.

Nancy, who was sitting in a car on the sidelines, went running down the field to see if he was okay. But Norman instantly jumped up and waved to her that he was all right. However, when she got to him, he said that he thought he had broken his wrist. He was taken by ambulance to the hospital where doctors diagnosed a broken left collarbone, shoulder, and right wrist broken in six places.

Norman was in the hospital for a couple of days, but hastily left one evening and showed up for his black-tie wedding anniversary party in an extended brace and cast from his wrist to his neck. Guests at the event could not believe that he had made it. But Norman said he didn't want to disappoint Nancy. "He acted as if there was nothing wrong with him," said one guest. "He danced with Nancy, enjoyed himself thoroughly, and was the last to leave the party."

~

IN MAY 1991, Chili's, Inc., was renamed Brinker International to reflect the scope and diversity of the corporation's operations. An executive task force, working with an outside agency, recommended the choice because of Norman's name recognition and the fact that it would be an easy name to remember. Five years later, in 1996, Brinker International was a billion-dollar company investing more than $200 million in capital expenditures yearly and employing more than sixty thousand people. It had grown from twenty-five restaurants in 1983–to five chains of more than five hundred restaurants serving in excess of two and a half million meals each week.

Not only was Brinker International in forty-four states, it had aggressively moved into a number of countries around the world, including: Australia, Japan, Singapore, Malaysia, Indonesia, Thailand, Great Britain, France, Egypt, Canada, and Mexico. In addition, the company had plans to expand energetically into new open markets elsewhere in the world.

Norman's penchant for growth, combined with his ability to inspire and care for people, resulted in a remarkable and long-standing pattern of financial success. For nearly three decades, from 1966 to 1996, Norman Brinker's companies had anywhere from one to one hundred restaurants under construction all the time. His orderly and aggressive *modus operandi* resulted in a 32 percent annualized compounded bottom-line increase from 1984 to 1994—the first ten years in which Norman led Chili's/Brinker International. It also resulted in twenty-nine consecutive years of bottom-line increases for the companies he led.

Of course, such a dramatic expansion also created some adverse effects for the company. The sheer reality of managing a fifty-thousand-person organization threatened to undo the very culture that had fueled its meteoric rise to prominence. "There is a very big tendency to start getting bureaucratic," said Norman, "of going by systems and not by feel, of losing the exuberance, the excitement, and the entrepreneurial flair. This must be avoided in every way possible."

Brinker worked hard to stay close to his customers and preserve a small-company atmosphere that involved and excited everyone. In order to perpetuate that goal, he found himself encouraging a leadership attitude. "Leadership in business," said Norman, "means being ahead of the game, having a vision, inspiring people—and taking a leadership role in your industry as well as your corporation."

To that end, Norman worked closely with Rick Berman in Washington, D.C., to create the Employment Policies Institute Foundation—a Washington, D.C., think tank devoted to accumulating, analyzing, and disseminating information regarding employment growth, job creation, and entry-level employment in the United States. The main idea was to be certain that the nation's laws and politics did not impede such growth. Norman reasoned that someone had to lead the restaurant industry's role in educating the federal government about issues that impacted individual opportunity—and that leadership should come from the private sector.

And closer to home, at Brinker, he set out on the path of pure leadership—delegating nearly all of the operations and management control of the corporation to members of the executive team. At the top of his list was his strong desire to *inspire* people to achieve their goals. He accomplished that objective by working with employees to set goals, to develop a culture of honesty, integrity, energy, and initiative—and by providing financial rewards and incentives.

"All I do is set an agenda and encourage people to set goals that come together in a larger common goal," he said. "I never tell folks what to do. It works the other way around. They commit to me. They say, 'Norman, with these resources, I can do such and such.' Then we all look for any better alternative. After adjustments, we move forward and then keep the team informed and up-to-date on a regular basis."

He also had zero tolerance for political infighting and back stabbing among people in the corporation—believing fully that if the leaders at the top did not allow negative behavior, it would not become part of the corporate culture. "Right off the bat, we committed to absolute trust and straight, honest talks and honest relationships," recalled Norman. "If any politics began to emerge, I really jumped on it. It was just not any part of our culture."

Moreover, employees in Brinker restaurants and at corporate headquarters were allowed to wear jeans and casual clothes—especially on Fridays. "We don't want anybody to feel uncomfortable," said Norman. He believed strongly that a more casual, informal nature actually increased communication. "If people feel comfortable where they are, don't feel intimidated, and are able to communicate freely and openly about what's on their minds—everything goes faster, easier, and with fewer complications."

Yet, even though the dress code was casual, Brinker International's organization maintained an orderly chain of command. Store managers reported to regional managers who reported to vice presidents, and so on. "A precise and logical chain of command gave us a structure that allowed for an orderly and efficient decision-making process. Casual dress helps keep open communication flowing. It's really a perfect combination."

In addition, as a matter of routine, Norman seldom summoned anyone to his office. "I don't send for people," he said. "For the most part, I go to other people's offices to see them instead of having them come to me. It's part of my culture." In essence, Norman knew that the other person would feel more comfortable in his/her own environment—and he would, therefore, stand a better chance of having his message get through and of receiving honest and straightforward feedback.

One of Norman's main principles of business leadership was to encourage people to enjoy the work they performed. In his mind, it made the entire corporate environment easier, more fun, and certainly more highly charged. "I believe in keeping people excited," he said. "We have a lot of fun at Brinker International—including parties, outings, and sporting events. It adds an incredible amount to our company."

Some of the annual events sponsored for employees included: an eighteen-hole miniature golf tournament through the halls and offices of corporate headquarters to promote team spirit and lift morale; a 5K and 10K run where more than six thousand employees participated in a benefit for hospitals; and a day-long event of activities surrounding the corporation's company picnic.

In addition, Brinker International employed several hundred people with disabilities, held annual events to feed homeless people, supported higher education and the arts, and was active in numerous charitable events, including the Susan G. Komen Foundation and the Scottish Rite Hospital for handicapped children. All this and more, because the corporation's chairman never forgot his mother's simple, yet pointed question: "What else are you doing, Norman— for your country, your community, your church?"

Clearly, Norman's caring nature enhanced his skill at leadership. As a matter of fact, the ability to care genuinely about others is a necessary trait for effective leadership. People do not follow leaders who don't care about the values, the wants and needs, the hopes and aspirations of those in the organization. They can quickly sense whether or not their leader's empathy is genuine.

Carl Hays, a vice president with Steak & Ale who went on to be a major franchisee for Outback Steakhouses, also noted Norman's skill and wisdom as a teacher. "Norman teaches you everything he knows," said Hays. "He helps you achieve your goals any way he can—selflessly and enthusiastically. There are probably a hundred managers and executives in the restaurant business who received an education from Norman that could not be bought anywhere else. He not only taught us about the restaurant business, but also about life, about ourselves. Norman helped us understand relationships, and how to make them work in terms of surrounding ourselves with the best people and then treating them with fairness and kindness."

Brinker had said frequently that he received great satisfaction from knowing that he influenced many thousands of young people who worked in his restaurants. "They've been able to go to college because of the jobs we've provided," he said, "and that certainly gave us all an extra sense of pride."

But more important, perhaps, was the culture that young people encountered at Norman Brinker's restaurants over the years. For many, it was a culture that they remembered and took with them into their later adult years. It is a culture of respect and high ethical behavior in which negative conduct is simply not tolerated.

When Norman walked into one of his restaurants, which on average was four or five times a week, he always looked for signs of that special culture on the bulletin boards, such as: photographs of people and their families; a fun contest of some sort; nifty quotations or sayings; and any other signs of exuberance and life. Ross Perot once observed that: "From the time he walks in, to the time he leaves, he takes a warm and personal interest in every person who works in the restaurant. He takes an interest in how the parking lot looks, in how the entrance looks, in how the flowers look, and in how the grass is kept. I've even seen him pick up a dishrag and bus tables on a busy day."

"Every time you visit an off-site location," said Brinker, "you ought to go to the back, thank people and tell them how good they're doing, and how much you appreciate their effort. The greater the distance between you and an employee in terms of your places in the hierarchy, the more important it is that you speak with them personally and show you care—really care."

Norm's presence at a restaurant always seemed to charge the atmosphere. And, conversely, he seemed to draw vigor and energy from the people around him. "Human contact is important to people. It's not only the most powerful and effective form of communication a leader can possess—it often inspires people into action. When you speak to folks personally, they really appreciate it, and frequently they will spread the word like wildfire."

Before Norman ever left a site, he generally took one last opportunity to canvas customers. In August of 1992, *The New York Times* reported that:

> *On any given day or night, Norman Brinker, a tall, balding man who comes off as a slightly befuddled tourist, can be found wandering the parking lots of America's restaurants. "Say, what kind of a restaurant is this?" or "How was the food?" he asks patrons as they leave.*

BRINKER PRINCIPLES

- Go out in the field. There is no substitute for spending time with the troops in their own environment.
- Compensation is a great motivator when leveraged properly.
- People do not fear change if they are involved in the planning process.
- As you expand operations, leverage your assets on a state-by-state and country-by-country basis.
- Listen to new ideas. One great success can pay for a hundred failures.
- Encourage continual renewal and reevaluation. Ask yourself what you can do better, quicker, and with more imagination.
- Inspire rather than dictate.
- Have zero tolerance for political infighting and back stabbing.
- People won't follow leaders who don't care.
- The greater the distance between you and an employee in terms of your places in the hierarchy, the more important it is that you speak with them personally and show you care.
- Human contact is the most powerful and effective form of communication a leader can possess.

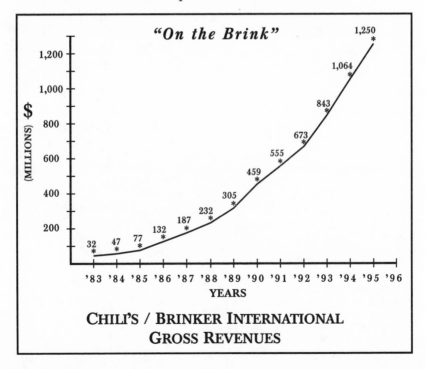

CHILI'S / BRINKER INTERNATIONAL
GROSS REVENUES

11
.

....

*"WELCOME BACK, NORMAN, WE
LOVE YOU."*

**BANNER ON THE OUTSIDE OF BRINKER
INTERNATIONAL HEADQUARTERS**

March 4, 1993

*"It's great to be here tonight. Actually, it's
great to be anywhere."*

NORMAN BRINKER,
to the Dallas Press Club, April 1994

*"I know I won't be playing polo any more,
but I'll ride again."*

NORMAN BRINKER,
1995

....

The Return

O n April 29, 1993–two days ahead of his May 1 goal, and six days before his scheduled corporate board meeting, Norman and Nancy hopped a commercial airplane for home. The flight went smoothly and silently.

As his plane touched down at Dallas/Fort Worth International Airport, Norman Brinker did not speak much because he was filled with emotion. He had come a long way to get back home–longer than any journey he had ever taken in his life. And Nancy was at his side. Actually, all the people who had helped him along the way were with him at that moment–Kathryn, Gene, Maureen, Bob, Ross, Cindy, Brenda, and Eric.

It was a forty-five-minute car ride from the airport to the Brinker home in north Dallas–and Norman enjoyed every second of it. "Oh, boy," he kept saying, "it's good to be home."

"When we arrived at the house," remembered Nancy, "Norman slowly walked in on his own power–without crutches or a cane. He wouldn't let anyone help him. I think he felt it was a symbolic moment, given everything he had been through."

"Well," he said as he stepped through the front door, "I'm not Superman, but I'm back."

Norman and Nancy spent the first four days at home in relative solitude. They celebrated quietly, got the house back in order, and read some of the thousands of get-well cards and letters that had piled up. Mostly, though, Norman saved his energy and prepared for the Brinker International board meeting scheduled for May 4 at corporate headquarters.

On that morning, Norman, without fanfare, arrived at headquarters five minutes before the scheduled start of the meeting at 9 A.M. He had not wanted a big fuss this day. As he walked into the boardroom, all the members gathered around him, patted him on the back, smiled and congratulated him. There was a genuine excitement in the boardroom—and a generous outpouring of affection for the man who led the company. Everyone sensed the importance of that event—the culmination of a remarkable, even miraculous recovery.

Norman greeted everyone with a handshake and called them all by name.

The first order of business was to reinstate him officially as chairman and chief executive officer. Ron McDougall, who had filled in over the last four months, graciously stepped aside. "Welcome back, Norman," he said. "You're a wonderful friend to us all, and it's great to have you here where you belong."

"There was not much overt celebration," recalled one board member. "Norman just wanted to get back into the groove without making too big a deal about it."

The next day, however, was a different story altogether. As Norman walked up to Brinker International headquarters, he noticed a large banner on the outside of the building that read: WELCOME BACK, NORMAN, WE LOVE YOU.

He had not told anyone when he was going to be there, but as he walked up to his office word spread like wildfire that he was back. Later that morning, when Margaret, Ron, and Nancy escorted Norman out to the ground floor patio, four hundred employees were waiting to welcome him with a sustained standing ovation.

Ron introduced Norman, in part, by reemphasizing the corporation's first quarter results: "Well, Norman, Brinker International had the single best quarter in the company's history. We all pulled together and did it for you. And most of all, we wanted you to be able to say that we did exactly what you would have done if you were here."

"When Norman began to speak," recalled Nancy, "many people just stood there and wept. He told them how much he loved them—and they showed him how much they loved him. It was a very emotional moment for everyone."

Norman was clearly moved, but he also was invigorated. He thanked those gathered for their hard work, and told them that they did exactly what he would have done if he had been able to be with them. Then, Norman mentioned two keys to his recovery. First and foremost, he said, was the wonderful outpouring of support he received from everybody. "I was determined to make it back, because all my friends are here," he told the crowd. "I love it here. I love this company. I love what I do. To me, it's not just a job—and that makes all the difference in the world."

The other key he discussed was not feeling sorry for himself. "Negative thinking is the first step backward," he said, "and that means no progress. I was more excited about the good things that were happening. I wasn't depressed about the negative side of things.

"The doctors told me I wouldn't be back anytime before the beginning of next January," he continued. "But I defied their expectations and returned by my goal of May 1. They didn't support me until five days before I left. And then they said, 'Good idea, Norm. Good idea.'"

That got a good laugh from the crowd.

"It's wonderful to be home," he concluded. "I feel marvelous—stronger and better and more excited."

$\sim$

NORMAN'S ROUTINE INCLUDED regular checkups with Dr. Phil Williams, who could document that his patient's strength and vibrancy were increasing almost daily. On one visit, after having taken a CAT scan that proved normal, Dr. Williams took Norman to meet the neuro-radiologist who had helped make the diagnosis in Florida a few days after the accident occurred. "Let's see you lean over," he said. So Norman leaned over. "Now, kneel down and pick something up." Norman did so.

"I cannot believe that anyone could recover like this," said the radiologist. "I agree," said Dr. Williams. "Norman, your recovery is nothing short of miraculous."

"Aww, I think you guys just read the X rays wrong," Norman quipped.

Right away, he began pressing his doctors to let him resume his previous activities. "Well, how about driving," asked Norman impatiently. "I think I can drive just fine."

"Well, I'm not sure about that, yet," said Dr. Williams. "You're not only going to need my permission to drive, you should also requalify for your Texas driver's license."

Norman then went home and told Nancy he had set a goal to be driving by his birthday on June 3. He immediately went out and signed up for some driving lessons with professional trainers so that he would be certain to pass the tests and drive well.

A few months later, he called Dr. Williams. "I knew what was coming," said Phil. "Every time Norman talked to me, he'd ask: 'How soon can I drive?'"

On this occasion, however, Norman asked the good doctor to take a ride so that he could see firsthand how well his driving was coming along. Dr. Williams agreed and drove over to the Brinkers'. With Norman behind the wheel, the two headed up north to Willow Bend where Norman drove on major highways, through residential neighborhoods, and parallel-parked.

"It was apparent that he could drive a car just fine," recalled Dr. Williams. "So I approved his license. When Brinker sets his mind to do something, he just goes out and does it."

Then Norman went down to the Department of Public Safety to take a driver's test. The officer who administered it told him that most people after such an accident would have just started driving again. "You made the effort to come down and get tested," said the officer. "I think that's great."

On June 3, his birthday, Norman passed his driver's test. "It was the most wonderful birthday present I ever had," he said.

And no one was happier about Norman getting his driver's license than Margaret Valentine, who had been chauffeuring him around. "He drove me crazy," she remembered. "'You're speeding up. Why don't you put your brakes on. Turn here. Park there.' Oh, I was so glad to get him out of my car.

"Of course," said Margaret, "Norman was stopped by a traffic cop for, what else but speeding. He paid the ticket and was so impressed with the officer's courtesy and professionalism that he later sent him a dinner pass."

∽

HAVING LEFT his rehabilitation team in Florida, Norman decided to build a completely new team when he returned to Dallas. He and Nancy interviewed and then hired physical and occupational therapists to help fine-tune Norm's walking, balance, and coordination. He continued having these two-hour sessions every day for a couple of months.

During this time, he spent half days at the office, gradually getting back into his work routine.

By January 1994, Norman was putting in at least eight-hour days at the office, often eating lunch at his desk and exercising religiously. He began each day at 6:30 A.M. working out in his home gym; walked two miles twice a day and swam once a day.

Before his accident, Norman was in the 99.6 percentile of fitness for his age. Exactly one year after the accident (January 21, 1994), following a comprehensive physical, his doctor (Dr. Sam Gibbons of the Cooper Clinic) ranked him in the 75th percentile.

Still walking with a limp and unable to run well, Norman looked at his doctor and exclaimed: "Gosh, Doc, if I'm in the seventy-fifth percentile, what do people in the fiftieth percentile look like?"

It wasn't long before Norman was rapidly moving around town and reestablishing all his old personal relationships. "When you have a serious accident like I had," he explained, "it makes you appreciate all that much more the friends you have and all the people who have really touched your life."

One Friday afternoon, having been in a particularly reflective mood, Norman decided to drive down to Brink's Coffee Shop for lunch with a few friends. It was still in business at the corner of Gaston and Carroll in east Dallas—and still owned by the same people (the Burns) who had purchased it from Norman back in 1968.

When Norman walked in, he saw the same tables, the same pictures of horses on the walls, and the same style menus. Everything was virtually unchanged. "It was like walking back in time thirty years," he commented.

Mrs. Lois Burns and her son, David, who were working as hostess and cashier, welcomed Norman with a hug and a handshake. When they showed him to his table, a waitress whom Norman had hired, walked up to him and gave him a big hug. "Nan," he said with a big grin, "you're still here."

"Sure am," she replied. "And guess what, I've got three grandchildren now. Can you believe it?"

From the menu, Norman ordered the "waistliner" (hamburger steak and cottage cheese). "Still on the menu after all this time," he said. "It was my first dish to help meet people's concerns about eating healthy foods."

When Norman finished his meal, the cook, Joe Gibbons, who could see all the customers from the open kitchen, came out and said hello. Norman stood up, shook his hand, and together they went over to the side and had a nice chat.

"He wanted to know how the meal was," said Norman. "He still wanted to make things better for his customers some twenty-five years later. And he told me he was glad to see me again. What a nice thing for him to say. I hadn't seen Joe in years. He's a great guy."

∼

IN AUGUST 1994, Ellie and Marvin Goodman came to Dallas to spend three days with Nancy and Norman. They hadn't seen their son-in-law in more than six months. "Norman, you look great," said Marvin when they first saw each other.

"Oh, thank you," he responded enthusiastically. "I'm feeling great, too. Making progress all the time."

"Gosh," said Marvin jokingly, "maybe we shouldn't have come, because it seems that every time we visit you, you have an accident."

The two men laughed heartily and recalled that the Goodmans had been there in Dallas during the 1983 polo accident just before he moved to Chili's; and during the 1989 fall in Florida when Norman soon after left the hospital to go to his anniversary party in a cast.

Then Ellie chimed in: "I recall thanking one of the doctors for helping put you back together again—and you know what his response was? He said, 'Norman is remarkable. I have never seen X rays with that number of breaks. I couldn't tell the old ones from the new ones!'

"As a matter of fact," she continued, "all your doctors in Dallas know me because of all those times I spent in the waiting rooms. You know, Norman, usually people are in an emergency room with kids that are four or five years old. But you are sixty-three years old now, and I hope you realize it's no longer acceptable for you to be putting yourself at such risk."

"Absolutely, I know that," said Norman. "And I won't forget, either, that you and Marvin traveled a hundred miles round trip each day from Fort Lauderdale to be with Nancy when I was in the coma and in rehabilitation. That really made a big difference. But don't you worry. I won't be riding any horses this time around."

The next day, Norman called his doctor in Dallas, Roby Mize, to get permission to be a little more active. "I already have my boat hooked up to go waterskiing," he told the doctor. "Is it all right?"

"Norman," responded Dr. Mize, "you spent nearly three weeks in a coma last February and now you want to go waterskiing this February?"

"Why, sure," responded Norman.

"Norman, is life okay without waterskiing?"

"Well, it's okay, but I don't want to stop being active."

"Well, then. Let's just wait another year or so and see how you're doing."

"Oh, okay," said Norman.

~

IN EARLY FEBRUARY 1995, a full two years after Norman's polo accident, he flew down to Palm Beach to watch the Challenge Cup tournament. As he walked up the steps to take his seat, he noticed that Dr. Sandy Carden was already sitting in the box right behind his own. Norman was very excited to see him and spend some personal time with him. So Norm sat down with the good doctor and began a conversation. It turned out to be a great opportunity to listen firsthand to Sandy's analysis of those traumatic days in January 1993.

"You know, Sandy," he began. "I've heard a lot of talk about the X rays. You were there right at the beginning. What did you think when you saw them? You studied them and carefully analyzed them, didn't you?"

"Yes, I did study them," replied Dr. Carden.

"Well, what did you think? Now that you can look back on it, tell me objectively how you saw it."

"Well, first of all, when I saw you walking up those steps, I got cold chills and goose bumps up my arm—because I never would have believed it. I never would have believed that this could have happened.

"When I looked at the X rays," continued Dr. Carden, "I was shocked and saddened, because I said to myself: 'One of my good friends is going to be gone. I've lost a very good friend.' I was just really torn apart about it."

"Well, I just don't understand it," said Norman. "Something in this equation is just not right. Maybe I wasn't hurt that bad. Maybe you just read the X rays wrong."

"No, I didn't read the X rays wrong," he replied, "but here's the thing. You never can tell what an individual's made from. Also, we couldn't tell exactly how much damage was caused by your injury. It was kind of like a car's battery cable. If it was all gone you would have been dead. You obviously had enough left to have impulses coming. And then your determination, physical fitness, and mental direction made it all work.

"I can tell you this," said Carden. "Of the four or five doctors who were there, not one of us has a patient with a similar injury who has made it through like you have. Not one. The best we can do is to have one patient who is fairly verbal in a wheelchair. That's the best. It's simply unbelievable to me that you only have a slight limp after what you've been through.

"As far as I'm concerned, Norman, you are a walking miracle."

"Well, Sandy," responded Norman, "many people had a lot to do with bringing me back. My family, my friends, the team of doctors and specialists, all really helped me succeed. And all the cards, the letters, the fact that so many people cared—that really did make a difference.

"You know, I've always cared about people before. But I never really realized just how much of a difference it could make in a person's comeback from a tough physical situation.

"That inspired me to do more and get better. And I know that caring inspires others as well. That accident proved it to me.

"So, now, I'm trying to pass that on to people.

"Our new motto at Brinker International is: 'We care.'

"And if I read an article and hear about a youngster being hurt, I'll write them a letter and sometimes send them some money—maybe four or five hundred dollars. The letters I get back from parents and kids say that they can't tell me how important it was to receive that and to know somebody else cared. But I know how important it was.

"You know, I've been very fortunate in life. I'm lucky I can do that for people."

"I think a lot of it must have had to do with your own tenacity and determination, as well, Norman," said Sandy.

"Yeah, I guess it did," replied Norman. "Basically, I just applied my business philosophy to the situation—only this time the goal was to rehabilitate myself. Amazingly enough, it worked. I feel great."

"Well, you know you're not completely one hundred percent yet," said Carden, ever the physician. "You just can't continue to live your life on the brink as you have in the past. And I certainly hope you're not going to be riding in any more polo tournaments."

"Sandy, I know I won't be playing polo any more," said Norman. "But I'll ride again."

∼

BACK IN DALLAS at the Brinker house, Nancy called out to Norman: "Dinner's almost on the table, honey."

"Okay," he replied, "Eric and I are just finishing up a little project."

Ten minutes later, Eric walked into the kitchen by himself.

"Where's your father?" asked Nancy.

"Oh, Mr. Perot came by, and the two of them went over to that place on Greenville Avenue to try out their new indoor artificial downhill ski ramp. He said he wouldn't be long."

"What!" she said. "When did this happen?"

"Well, they just walked out the door," said Eric.

Nancy went running to the back porch just in time to see Norman and Ross pulling out of the driveway.

"NORMAN!" she called out at the top of her lungs. "NORMAN! You come back here right now!"

As they drove away, a smiling Norman rolled down his window, waved good-bye, and said: "I'll be right back."

The Brinker Leadership Philosophy

THE FOUNDATION

....

Dream the Idea
"There's nothing more valuable in the world than an idea—especially when it involves creating and perpetuating something of lasting value."

Begin With the End in Mind
"Have a real sense of direction. Visualize graphically where you want to go. Then it is critical that you take a long-term view of how you want to achieve your vision. When it comes right down to it, I do one thing: I have a vision, then I create an atmosphere that involves the people in that vision."

Get Out in the Field, Get to Know People, and Involve Everybody
"There's no substitute for spending time with people in their own environment. You not only meet everybody personally, you are able to see and hear for yourself what's going on."

Create the Culture
"Work together with employees to develop a 'can-do' culture of honesty, integrity, energy, and initiative. Create a casual environment where people feel uninhibited to communicate their feelings and ideas freely. Business is people, and it reflects the morality or mentality of people, no better, no worse. I wouldn't consider doing business with anyone unethical, and the only problem I've ever had is when I inadvertently did business with someone who was not absolutely honest."

Pick Your Team; Surround Yourself With the Best and the Brightest
"Look for people who are not only individual stars but can also work in a team environment; for those who have a lot of energy; for those who are smart. Remember, sinners can repent, but stupidity is forever."

A SENSE OF ACHIEVEMENT

Seek to Understand Before You Seek to Be Understood
"Listen, Listen, Listen–to employees and customers. Create an environment of 'bottoms-up' communication rather than only 'top-down.' And when in doubt, listen to your customers. They'll tell you what to do."

Be Decisive
"Decisiveness in an organization creates a dynamic and vibrant atmosphere. People move with a spring in their step and purpose in their direction. I love competing against autocrats, because sooner or later they will make bad decisions. A smart, balanced team will always win over time."

Set Clear, Definable Goals and Be Team-Oriented
"Always have a goal. Goals unify people, motivate them, focus their collective talent and energy. Work with your team to set shared goals. Quantify and benchmark progress on a regular basis. If you don't have a road map, or know where you are–you may be there already."

Delegate and Empower
"You can achieve so much more by empowering people to achieve on their own. Don't be too hands-on."

Leverage Assets, People, and Time
"Maximize capital assets by creating partnerships and joint ventures. Expand and outflank the competition by utilizing the expertise of locals who know their area, their market, and their customers."

Be Growth-Oriented
"Insist on making specific progress by having an unmitigated desire to get things done. Of course, one of your goals should be to increase the bottom line each year."

Take Risks
"Don't be afraid to risk everything to pursue your passion in life. Allow people to try and fail. Mistakes can be tolerated, inertia cannot."

Encourage Innovation

"Always look for ways to do things better. Apply and encourage imagination, initiative, creativity, and ingenuity."

Be Flexible and Change-Oriented

"Stay a step ahead of the competition by observing, anticipating, and acting on the latest trends in your industry. Renew and reinvigorate your operations on a regular basis. Don't be afraid to change."

Take a Leadership Role in Your Industry

"Leadership means not only keeping your organization on top. It also means keeping your industry healthy and vibrant. Someone needs to anticipate trends and fight back against unthinking, unwarranted intrusion. It might as well–and, perhaps, should–be you."

Seize Opportunities When They Arise

"Many people have told me that I've been lucky. But I believe that the harder you work, the luckier you get. And timing certainly has an effect on your luck."

CARE ABOUT THE HUMAN SIDE OF LIFE

Study Human Nature
"Strive to understand people and learn to read body language. Take note of how people react in various situations. Remember that a company is a community of people, and when it comes together, it's remarkable what can happen."

Build Lasting Personal Relationships
"I never like it when only one person makes all the money. I don't know that people lose, they just don't gain. Create *win-win* situations and partnerships with others. Proper relationships will grow stronger as time goes by–providing you put something into them. Strive for 'psychological commitments.' And remember that personal human contact is the most powerful and effective form of communication a leader can possess."

Inspire Rather Than Coerce
"If I tell you what to do, then the task is my responsibility, not yours. But if I inspire you to act on your own, the responsibility and results are yours. The difference in dedication is phenomenal."

Give Credit Where Credit is Due
"It's amazing how much you can achieve if you don't worry about who gets the credit. Acknowledge and show genuine appreciation when a good job is done. Accept responsibility when things go wrong."

Share the Wealth
"Pay your people well. Institute generous profit-sharing and reward performance."

Help People Grow
"People either shrivel or grow. Commit to helping people help themselves. Be a mentor to others."

Give Something Back to the Community
"My mother always asked me: 'Son, what else are you doing? What are you doing for your community, your country, your church?' Getting involved both politically and philanthropically will repay you in a thousand ways you never even knew existed."

COMMON THREADS

....

High Energy, Physical Fitness, and a Competitive Nature
"Be physically fit and possess a strong competitive spirit–have a sense of urgency. You should draw energy from those around you. Remember, if you're thinking about it, your competitor may already be doing it."

Curiosity
"Watch people who both win and finish second. Learn from the winners–and learn what the difference is between them and the runners-up. Learn continually. Learn from your mistakes. Let your curiosity lead you forward."

Perseverance
"Determination and perseverance make the difference between winners and losers. Don't let others tell you it can't be done. Never, ever give up–and never give in."

Self-Confidence and Optimism
"*Know* yourself. *Believe* in yourself. *Trust* your judgment. And always remember that happiness is a habit–as is attitude."

Have Fun
"Have a lot of kid in you. If you have fun at what you do, you'll never work a day in your life. Make work like play–and play like hell."